LIFE OF THE

GORGEOUS

BUTTERFLY

TENICA NICOLE COFIELD

ISBN-13: 978-1-970079-34-0

Published and edited by:
Opportune Independent Publishing Co.
113 N. Live Oak Street
Houston, TX 77003
(832) 263-1700
www.opportunepublishing.com

DEDICATION

To ALL of my QUEENS who are living in fear,

It's time to step out into the unknown and live your PURPOSE in life. Don't be ashamed to share your past story or present stories with others. Trust and believe you're not alone. God approves sharing your testimonies, not your business. Look in the mirror and see what God sees in you. No matter what you're going through or what you have been through, love yourself the way God loves you. Study and learn your worth. You are beautiful and very much deserving. And always remember you are a Queen!

"Blessed is she who believed that the Lord would fulfill His promises to her."
—Luke 1:45 (NIV)

ACKNOWLEDGMENTS

To My Son's, Travion, Antonio Jr., and Tyeion,

My life, my heartbeat, and my SONshines, I do not know where I would be without all three of you. You boys are one of the greatest gifts God ever gave me. Thank you guys for supporting my dream and loving me. Mommy loves you guys ABUNDANTLY.

To My Beautiful Mother Patricia A. Thomas-Brown,

Without God and you there wouldn't be no me. I admire your strength, wisdom, knowledge, and kindness. Thank you for teaching your baby girl how to Sincerely pray...I love you for a LIFETIME.

To My Dad, Jerry J. Hannah Sr.,

Thank you for teaching your baby girl how to always carry herself like a lady and making sure her appearance is always ON POINT no matter what... I love you Pops.

To My Stepfather, Joseph W. Brown,

Thank you for teaching me who God is, who I am, and what God sees in me. Thank you for always letting me know that I am Strong, Powerful, and ABLE! I love you more than you would ever know.

Shaleah,

Thank you for purchasing "LOTGB". I pray my book touch your heart and inspire you

Jennise Green

INTRODUCTION

I decided to write a book about my whole entire life because I experienced so much as a child, teen, and Adult. I wanted to share my life story and how I became a Gorgeous Butterfly. It's a lot of GORGEOUS Butterflies out there that hasn't yet transformed from the Caterpillar. Some of you guys have already transformed. My amazing story will give you the inside look on how I finally got wings and became confident enough to fly high and freely from all my troubles, bad habits, and pain.

"God is in the midst of her; she shall not be moved: God shall help her, and that right early."
—Psalm 46:5 (KJV)

TABLE OF CONTENTS

CHAPTER 1
WHO AM I?

I am Tenica Nicole Hannah a GORGEOUS butterfly that God created on April 19, 1982, in Tallahassee, Florida, also known as the "Capital City." My parents are Patricia A. Thomas and Jerry J. Hannah Sr. I always tell myself that God knew exactly what he was doing when he created me.

My mother has a total of five children: two boys and three girls. My father has four children: three girls, and one boy. On both sides of the family, I am the baby girl. I am the spoiled brat of the family, as many say, and I agree!

Believe it or not, my mother had two abortions and three miscarriages after her fourth child. Wow, can you imagine having that many abortions and miscarriages? That's a lot for one person to have. That definitely can take a toll on a person's body. After my mother's last miscarriage, she thought that she was done, but God said differently. Not before too long my mother was pregnant again with another baby. She was so scared and nervous.

God being the God he is, allowed her to be beyond blessed with one more, which was a girl. And that was ME! I would consider myself to be a miracle baby. I was born into this world after abortions and miscarriages, and not to mention I was born with severe asthma and bronchitis. Asthma was pretty rough for me and is one of the things you wouldn't want your child to have. I had a rough childhood full of illness from birth until I reached about 12. This was a lot to deal with because I was in and out of the hospital all the time. It was so aggravating and very painful many of the times. For example, throwing up from my nose had become regular for me at that time.

I spent more days in the hospital then I did at home, daycare or school. I had to take medicine all the time throughout the day and with the majority of my food. Which was one of the ways my mother could get me to take it, anyway; She had to trick me. One of the reasons why I do not like applesauce today is that I still can taste the medicine in it.

There were a series of things that I was affected by.

If I got too hot from running or playing, I would start wheezing. It was to the point that I couldn't really enjoy my younger days because I was so limited to certain activities. My mother missed work a lot for me, but thank God my grandmother, "Ollie Mae," could step in and help at times. She took care of me, helped me use my asthma machine, and made sure I took my medicine on time. I can remember those days like they were yesterday.

The devil tried to take me from my mother, but the Lord kept me around longer. So many long nights of not feeling well, couldn't breathe out my nose or mouth. My body was so weak all the time; I was so little and couldn't do much. I don't know if anyone ever experienced asthma-like this, but I had it very bad. I spent so many days out of school that I had to repeat kindergarten. Being a year behind was not good! But the school didn't care; they held me back anyway.

My friends were wondering why I was still in the same grade they had just left. But that was my life. Even though I was young, it sucked for me. I was so happy when I started to grow out of it, but my mother was still cautious with me. I went from having asthma attacks all the time to not really having them at all once I was 12 years old.

I was happy because I didn't like being in the house all the time, not being able to go outside and play with my friends or cousins. Not saying I didn't enjoy being spoiled by my grandmother and watching her two favorite shows, "The Stories" and "Murder She Wrote."

I can remember one day I was at school and got in trouble with my teacher. She told me she was going to call my mom. I told her, "So, I don't care! I can be home with my grandma watching soap operas!"

That tickled my mother and grandmother to death but, my teacher didn't find it to be very funny. Obviously, the joke came from me spending so much time with my grandmother rather than being at school.

My family really knew how serious my asthma was; they would all looked out for me. But it wasn't the only thing I suffered from growing up. When I was in the fourth grade, at Leonard Wesson Elementary school I suffered from minor things like dyslexia, but I didn't know I had it at the time. Other kids used to make fun of me all the time. Some used to call me "slow." I had problems in school with comprehension and remembering the things that I read. My teachers use to fuss at me all the time because she thought I was pretending. I had a serious disorder that involves difficulty in learning to read and write.

Sometimes my teacher called me out on purpose to make me read out loud. I used to cry every time. She would even get a ruler and hit me on my knuckles whenever I messed up or I missed a word. I don't know if it was because I was always talking in class that made her feel like I was playing when I didn't pronounce words right.

I think that's why I used to be the class clown and make my classmates laugh—to take their attention off of me not being able to do my work properly. I don't think my friends ever really caught hold. They just called me names. Some of my teachers were getting very concerned. They had several meetings with my mother to discuss my issues.

They would go over the work with me several times, but I still didn't get it. My mother took notice and decided to take me to get tested for dyslexia because that's what one of my teachers recommended. I was very nervous when I took the test, but I had no choice. The test came back showing that I had it. I never let anyone know. I was too ashamed, and until this day, nobody knows.

I had to get glasses in elementary school and I didn't want to wear those things. They were so ugly, big and purple. They were the worst glasses a child could wear, in my opinion. I was so mad that my mother made me get those glasses. I felt like a slow little girl with big purple glasses. Plus, finding out that I had dyslexia didn't make it any better. I had to figure out other ways to be cool, and that's why I started telling jokes all the time trying to be funny. On top of that, I had two big bucked front teeth... none of that went together at all. I wanted braces so badly, but my mother would never get me any because she didn't care for them and didn't want to pay for them either.

My siblings don't even know that my mother took me to get tested because I didn't want anybody knowing anything. I was ashamed of everything. Deep down inside I felt like a loner as a little girl. I wanted so badly to be pretty and popular. My self-esteem was super low growing up.

I lived with my mother, sister Lisa, and my brother Jordan. I don't remember too much about my big sister Sasha and big brother Jason because they were raised by their father's mother, which is their grandmother. I know they came around a couple of times, but not much. Jordan, Lisa and I have the same father, and Sasha and Jason have the same father, but we all have the same mother. So, growing up we pretty much were separated from our other siblings all of the time.

To be honest, I don't know exactly what went on and why we were separated like that. As I got a little older, I heard stories that my sister and brother were taken away from my mother while she was at work by their grandmother. But whatever happened, I wished it never did because siblings are always supposed to stay with their mother and together with their other siblings. But throughout life, we began to be around each other more.

My parents divorced a little bit after I was born. I asked my mother, "Why did you guys wait until I was born?"

Every child wants to grow up living with both parents. But, they went through things way before I was thought of. My mother used to tell me that that's life and things happen, whatever that meant! It didn't have anything to do with her kids; it was her. I guess she didn't want me to think that the divorce was about me and my siblings. I didn't feel that way. I just wanted to know why they would wait until I was born to get a divorce. I would've loved to experience having both parents in the same household that were married.

At that time, I felt love from both parents, so it really didn't matter to me. I loved my family, especially my cousins. We didn't need friends; we had each other to play with at my grandmother's house. That's where everybody stayed, and celebrated all of the holidays and birthdays. Those were some of the best days of our lives.

My grandma, "Ollie Mae," was a sweet lady and everyone just loved her dearly. She was well known for her homemade sweet potato pies and delicious cakes. She could make any flavor cake you could think of. To me, she was the best cook who ever lived. Everything she made or touched was delicious. Not only did she make desserts, but she also made great soul food! Everything was always made from scratch. We could always depend on her to cook a whole meal, and she didn't need any help in the kitchen.

My grandma, "Ollie Mae," passed away when I was little, and things have not been the same for the Johnson family since. We no longer celebrate holidays together like we used to and should do. I don't know why in African American families they stop celebrating holidays and birthdays when the ancestors pass away. Things should always remain traditional and the legacy should live on.

There's nothing like a family gathering with lots of food, laughs, fun, and memories. Especially since everyone in my family can cook like my grandmother, well, the majority of us. So, I don't see what the problem is. A lot of the family members picked up her way of cooking. She taught everyone well when it came to cooking. We surely miss her! A lot of things would be better than they are today, if she was still here.

Even my best friend/cousin passed away and left this world. They both were my favorite and took a part of me when they left. My cousin was like my sister and my best friend. I loved her so much. It shattered my heart when she passed away. I couldn't even go to her funeral. I couldn't take seeing her like that.

I especially miss her beautiful smile. She was sweet, inside and out. I always loved when she would come over and stay weekends with me at my house. Her father and my mother were brother and sister. I never saw her get mad or upset. She was always smiling and laughing. This was not easy for me at all, and the thought of it makes me sad. Till this day Losing family can be very damaging. It can cause many life-changing circumstances for people. I would do any and everything in my power to have my cousin and my grandmother back, but I understand that they're in a better place smiling down on us.

I know things would be completely different in the Johnson family if my grandma were here still. I guess it's selfish for us to want our family to live forever and never leave us, but we always do. My cousin knew me better than anybody. I am a sweet person, and some understand me, and others do not. To some, I have a "smart mouth"; others see it as me keeping it real. But I tell you I am one of the coolest, sweet, crazy, funny, sassy, rude, and encouraging friend you could ever have. All of that in one!

Some things that people may not know about me is that I love singing, dancing, cooking, reading, writing and doing hair. I've always wanted to travel a lot and become a fashion designer—that was my No.1 goal when I was a little girl—and to open up a boutique of my own. I used to tell my mother that I just want to graduate and move out of town to do fashion of some sort. I had my life all planned out! I was like any other little girl with a big dream and goal.

I come from a family that really didn't achieve goals. We just live life! We all grew up in the projects and stayed together in one apartment. When it came to a family member needing somewhere to stay, we definitely stuck together.

I remember staying with a couple of family members, at my grandmother's home before. She didn't care. She'd let any and everybody stay at her house. Even though my family grew up in the projects, we were raised going to church and were taught to go every Sunday. She made sure all of her kids, grandkids and, great-grandchildren would go to church on Sundays. She even made us participate in church activities.

We did everything with the church and went on all of the trips. On Sunday morning, you were guaranteed a cooked breakfast with homemade biscuits. That's what really got us up and ready to go to church. We all knew that Saturday and Sunday were grandma's "homemade biscuit" days. We looked forward to that for sure.

My grandmother also raised us not to do chores on Sundays because that's the Lord's day. My grandmother did not play about church and the rules extended to other's houses as well. If you needed to wash clothes, you better had done it before Sunday came. If not, they wouldn't get washed until Monday or after. You couldn't even sleep in at her house on the weekends. She would wake the whole house up early. "Get up and clean up!" She would yell.

We used to be mad about that because we used to stay up late, so we were not trying to get up early at all. That went for the adults too. She didn't care; you were going to respect her house and her rules, or else. We should really cherish those type of values because there were so many moments that we cannot get back. So many of us praying and wishing that we could have our loved ones back when we need to enjoy them while they're here.

Lots of times I wish I could go back to those good days when kids were kids and family was family. Nothing but love being spread with lots of fun and laughter. My grandmother was the glue that kept everything together. Everyone knows that without glue, it will not stick. Things have changed so much. Thank God for memories because they last a lifetime.

My grandmother left a huge impact on a lot of people, and it was good. That's something that we all should want to do when we leave this world.

~In Loving Memory~
Ollie Mae Cooper- Johnson
(1921-1997)

Markisha Johnson
(1982-2000)

Leroy Johnson
(1956-2016)

CHAPTER 2
MY MOTHER'S ADDICTION

There are things in life that we try not to remember and other things you don't mind remembering. One of the things I tried to forget is that my mother was addicted to crack cocaine when I was a little girl. She was on drugs so bad and mostly everybody around her was too. My father and some family members were on some type of drugs as well.

I was young, but I could remember my environment and surroundings. Drinking and smoking drugs was never a stranger to my life growing up. My father was on drugs but I never witnessed him doing it but I did witness him drinking alcohol all of the time. I used to hear whispers about it though. I knew for sure my mother was using drugs because I was always around her. People used to talk so bad about my mother and call her all kind of names like the ones you hear often: Crack head, Dope head, and Rock head. It's sad but it's true.

Yes, she did drugs but she also was a hard worker. She worked her butt off after her divorce from my father. My father was a hard worker too. He did his thing & race cars on the side. His name "Jerry Hannah" ring bells back in the day around Tallahassee and Miccosukee, Fl. His cars was his life and we all knew that for sure. He didn't play about his cars

21

and he kept them clean everyday! My grandmother Ollie Mae didn't care too much for my father. She always thought he was a big show off. My mother & my father use to get talked about a lot, especially about the drugs. But No matter how much drugs she did, she always went to work. She was a true working woman. But when night came, those were the times I didn't like because she would go out and find drugs. She'd come back with crack, go into the room and smoke it. Sometimes her friends would come over to smoke it with her.

My sister Lisa and I were the only ones staying with my mother at that time. Lisa used to be in her room with the door closed, but not me. I was nosey and I wanted to see what was going on. I used to be out in the hallway and soon as my mother closed her room door to get high, I used to throw shoes, toys, or whatever I could at the door. Reason being, I did not like my mother doing drugs, so I did every-thing I could to try to stop her.

When she used to leave the house at night or anytime, to go to the crack house I would go after her to find her. Of course, I would go to every drug house I knew or could think of to see if my mother was there. Deep down inside I was scared but I remained brave enough to go looking for my mother. It didn't matter what time of day or night it was, I was out looking for her. I wouldn't stop until I found her.

Her crack using friends used to look at me as if I were crazy and say things like, "Little girl, what are you doing here?"

I would tell them I'm looking for my mom, Pat. When my

mom walked outside and saw me, she used to say, "Nica!"

I would reply, "I came looking for you... Mommy, please come home."

I would cry out to her and tell her that I wasn't leaving till she came home. I would sit outside that house waiting on my mother to finish. I was only seven years old and I loved my mother so much that I couldn't sleep without her in the house with me.

I never could comprehend how some family members could talk about her so badly but would never help her get off of drugs. I don't know how long my mother was on drugs before she had me but from the age of seven to twelve, I can remember.

Whenever we got things for Christmas, my mother used to sell it for drugs. She used to take our money and use it to buy drugs with. My sister Lisa used to get so upset with me because I would just give my mother all of my money. I would, but not Lisa! She used to fight with our mother over her money because she was not giving up her money for drugs.

I didn't want my mother using drugs, but I didn't like how she got when we didn't give her our money. I was young and really didn't understand half of the stuff that was going on in my life. I realized my mom was doing drugs and very often.

Lisa used to yell at me all of the time, telling me I'm so stupid for giving her my money. Lisa got so tired of our mothers' drug use that she packed up her stuff and went to go stay with our father. They tried to get me to go stay with him as well, but I said no. I wasn't going to leave my mother alone, especially since she was on drugs. Plus, I cared. So, I stayed with my mother and was so afraid and felt so alone when my sister Lisa left me.

One of my other siblings, Jordan, had got in some trouble and ended up in prison for attempted murder in 1996. He was only 16 years old at the time. Before he got locked up, he used to be out in the streets living that street life and making fast money. Even though he was young, he always looked out for me. No matter what he did out in the streets, he always made sure that I had clothes and food to eat.

I don't know exactly what happened to him and why he grew up so fast, but he did. I guess we all kind of had to. At a young age, I had to pick my own clothes out for school and do my hair by myself. That's honestly how I learned how to do hair and weave.

Lisa didn't know how sad I was when she left me, but I just couldn't leave my mother. I was only a little kid, what was I supposed to do? I felt my mother needed somebody by her side to show her that she was still loved no matter what.

I wasn't close with my big sister Sasha and my other big brother Jason, but they were around, just not in my life like they should've been. Maybe because of how things were between them and my mother. I don't know how their relationship was with Jordan since he was closer to their age.

So, I didn't have anyone to look after me once Lisa left and my brother Jordan got locked up. Lisa and my dad weren't getting along so well, so she decided to move back into the house with us. Unfortunately, my mother was still on drugs and nothing had changed. Lisa was so confused that she started staying between our house and sometimes our grandmother's house.

My mother started working for this new moving company, Atlas Van Line. She was then mostly on the road traveling out of state for work and my grandmother used to watch me while my mother travel.

There was a lady named Mary that moved in next to my grandmother in South City projects. She became my guardian angel and I asked her would she be my godmother, so she took me in as her own. Mary only had one daughter, but she loved me and I loved her. We had gotten so close to one another that I was with her all the time. She bought me clothes and shoes, she even did my hair with bows...

Everything that she did for her daughter, she did for me as well. My mom actually loved her because she saw the genuine love she was giving me as if I was her biological daughter. My mom didn't mind because she always wanted me to have the best and she loved that Mary was giving it to her baby girl.

There were a lot of things that she couldn't give me because she was on drugs, but she knew that Mary could. I spent so much time with her that it felt as if that was my home since my mother was traveling a lot at that time. While my mother was working her new job she started dating this guy who was working with her. He was actually the driver of the truck and she helped him out with his loading and unloading. He was a very nice and sweet guy that loved my mother and her kids too, especially me.

I thought that would be a distraction from her using drugs but it wasn't long before he was buying her drugs and beer all of the time. These bad roads just seemed to not go away, around or out of my mother's life.

I always used to think and ask myself is anybody going to help her? Whenever I stay at my My godmother or my grandmother's house, my sister Lisa would stay too. Lisa and I would go to school from there and after school, we would go to the Boys & Girls Club of Big Bend in the neighborhood. We loved going to that place! We met new friends in the neighborhood and it was just a place for us to play with other kids, do arts and crafts and a lot of other fun activities.

One day, Lisa and I were at the Boys and Girls Club and the Department of Children and Families came in to talk to us. I didn't know exactly who they were and what they wanted with me and my sister Lisa. They asked us about my mother being on drugs, abusing us, and not taking care of us. We didn't know what to do or what to say. My hands were shaking, my voice was cracking and my heart was beating fast. We told them that our mom wasn't on drugs, nor was she abusing us and yes she took good care of us. Even Lisa agreed to everything that I was saying and she also was telling the same story.

They looked at us to check us out and everything, then they left. Later on, we went back to my grandmother's house and told her what had happened and then my mom when she came. She was so upset and had already known who had called but we had no idea at that time. Come to find out it was my big sister Sasha; she had called them on our mother because of the issues they were having and them not getting along in reference to the past.

I've always been a big cry baby so I was crying badly because it seemed like they were about to take us from our mother. I definitely didn't want them to take us from my mother. I couldn't imagine being away from her and I felt it deep down in my heart that she needed me with her at all times.

Before they could fully get further into the case, my mother decided to help herself. She joined a rehabilitation for drugs and alcohol. Knowing she had to make a change because she didn't want to lose us. She knew no one was going to help her and that upset her, so she had to make the right decision to go get help.

When she started going to the meetings and being around other people in the same situation, it actually helped her to want to change, do and be better and stop doing drugs. Things definitely started changing for the better quickly. The way my mother was starting to change made things seem so easy. I've always believed that she wanted to stop doing drugs, but she didn't know how to because of her environment.

One thing I can say is that my mom never did lie to me about getting off of drugs. Just how some addicts would tell their families, then do the opposite. Whenever she saw me cry or when I would go to those houses to ask her to stop doing it, she would say, "Baby, you're going to be okay and I'm okay."

27

But once she started going to the rehabilitation, she told me that she's getting off of drugs. And her actions matched her words. Lisa didn't like the old her and she definitely didn't like the new her they really started not getting along even more. My mother was changing daily and there were rules being made and Lisa didn't agree with them. So, Lisa moved out again to go stay with our father.

That particular time, my dad came and took me too. Even though I enjoyed spending time with my father, I didn't want to be without my mother. I didn't understand why he came to take me, especially since my mom was going through rehab and getting help.

My dad's house was a place I only liked to go on the weekends. He would take us around his side of the family, which I loved to go play with my cousins so it was nice. We didn't see them often, so my dad tried to take us around as much as possible. It was always a great time with our other side of the family.

My dad loved me and I was his baby girl, but it seems like the relationship between my mom and him wasn't good at all. He started to treat me badly and take his frustrations out on me that he had with my mother. Nobody knew but my dad was starting to be mean to me a lot about the little things. I used to think that it was something that he had against me, but I couldn't understand that because I was his baby girl and I was expecting him to spoil me as my mother spoiled me.

At that time, I wasn't seeing my mother as much but I was missing her like crazy and I was always worried about her.

One day, my dad was at work and I called my mother to come pick me up from my father's house. So she did. When my dad found out, he was pissed. My mother and him were going back and forth arguing over me and my mother had me to tell him what I told her which he didn't take very well.

I told him that I didn't want to stay with him; I wanted to stay with my mother. He was mad and we didn't talk for a while and he didn't come around to see me. My sister stayed with my dad. She was always willing to go stay with him until he pissed her off. Ever since that day my mother came to pick me up, I stayed by her side all the way through rehab and everything else too. I've been by her side from the beginning to the end. I am definitely a "Mommy's Girl."

There is no love like a mothers love and I cherished that no matter how bad things were or seemed. By my mother being in rehab, she became friends with the director, Miss Kathy, who was also a recovering drug addict. Miss Kathy invited my mother and me to her church, which we actually began to go there often. My mother fell in love with the church and the church family.

Wherever my mother went, I went too. There were no more nights where she left me anywhere alone; we were stuck together like glue. The director's brother, Mr. Joe, had moved up from Fort Lauderdale, Florida, and he was also a recovering drug addict too. I knew a lot of her rehab family because I used to go with her sometimes to events that they were having.

In the process of my mother getting herself together, she decided to give her life back to Christ. Chaires Community

Apostolic Holiness Church became our new Church home. Everyone there was so welcoming that we were all like family.

Mr. Joe and my mother started hanging out and then eventually dating. I didn't like him dating my mother and I didn't like him being with my mother all the time. The only time they were OK was if they were in group meetings or the rehab house. She even brought him home to my grandmother's house.

They were spending so much time together and I could see her looking and feeling so much better. But I felt like he was trying to take my mother away from me and we were all that one another had. When she brought him to the house one day, she told me to say "Hey" but all I could do was stare at him. He spoke to me but I didn't say anything back. They went out on the porch to eat their lunch and my cousin and I looked through the window at them.

Mr. Joe didn't have any teeth in his mouth and we were laughing and picking at him. We thought that it was the funniest thing ever, we couldn't stop laughing and peeking out the window. They had some chicken from Popeye's and whenever he would try to bite his chicken, we would laugh. Mr. Joe got so mad and embarrassed that he told my mother to close the curtains and for us to stop looking out of the window. My mother didn't see my cousin and I because when she turned her head we would hide.

When my mother came into the house she told us to sit down and stay out of the curtains. She instructed us to leave Mr. Joe alone and that it wasn't funny. We didn't care because we knew my mother wasn't going to do anything to us.

I opened the curtains again and started making faces like him; Pretending I had food in my mouth and chewed like him with no teeth. We were rolling! Mr. Joe got so angry that he got up, took his food and left. I guess I needed to do more than that because he kept coming around and they continued to date.

My mother did six months of rehab before she could graduate. I was so proud of her and couldn't believe it. Even my sister Lisa came and was proud of her as well. She wasn't doing any drugs throughout the process and I didn't see her drink or buy any beer. Her graduation day was a huge achievement and made our day. Mr. Joe had graduated from the program too. Some family and friends but not many came out to see her.

After about a year of my mother being clean and doing well, Mr. Joe asked her to marry him. My sister Sasha and mother was in a better place. She was coming around a lot more. Next, it was wedding bells. My mother got married and had a small southern bell wedding at Chaires Church I called it "The little house on the Prairie." It was official Mr. Joseph W. Brown and Patricia A. Brown were married and he was my new stepfather.

I had no choice but to like him and accept it because now he was a part of my life. The wedding was beautiful with friends and some family. My mother made all of her girls her bridesmaids. It was the beginning of a new life for my mother. Everything about her special day was amazing. God did a huge turnaround in her.

Tenica Cofield

CHAPTER 3
WELCOME TO MOTHERHOOD

I was only 14 years old when I lost my virginity in the eighth grade. My first time was with my middle school crush, Demarcus Chambers. All the girls loved him. He was a shorty, but such a cutie. Everybody knew I was crazy about him, especially my sister Lisa.

One day, I was hanging out with two of my cousins, Kyra and Tyra. We weren't blood cousins, but they were my sister Sasha cousins, so we called one another cousins too. They were much older than me, but I loved hanging out with them. They were so much fun and very cool.

Kyra was dating a dude that was good friends with Demarcus. One day, she asked me if I wanted to ride with her and Tyra over to the boys' house in the Meadows Trailer Park. Of course, I said yes, because I wanted to see Demarcus and he was there. So we all were just chilling at their house. Demarcus asked me to come into his room with him, and so I did. At first, I wanted to say no, but I couldn't let him know, or think I was scared.

Everybody that was in the living room were older; I was the youngest person there. I couldn't let them think I was a little

33

girl, even though I was at the time just trying to hang out with the older crowd. We went into his room, sat on the bed, and he went straight to the point. He began kissing me on my neck and in my mouth. I don't know if he noticed, but I had no clue what I was doing. I pretty much had to follow his lead. You can tell he wasn't a stranger to it the way he was kissing and handling me.

He started by taking my clothes off and then he took his clothes off too. He grabbed a condom and put it on and I thought to myself, Oh no! This is really about to happen.

The first thing that came to mind is that I'm not old enough and my mother is going to kill me, but I couldn't stop him because, once again, I didn't want him to think I was acting like a little kid. Also, it could've messed up my chance of him liking me.

One thing led to another and then it started. It hurt and I had no clue what I was doing. I was only doing it because he started it and asked me to. I hadn't been sexually active at all, so that was my very first time.

We never dated. It was always a huge crush and passing by one another when we were out. I must be honest. I was so ready for it to be over, and I couldn't wait to leave. I couldn't believe what had just happened. My body was numb after a while. I don't think I was able to feel anything else. I was happy when he finished.

He asked did I like it and I said, "Yes." But the answer was really no. When we went back into the living room, my cousins were looking at me smiling. I didn't say a word. Also, when we got in the car to leave I didn't say anything on the way back to the house. My cousins asked if we had sex, but I didn't answer because I'm sure they knew we did.

Later that week, I went to my godmother's house. She and I were very close, and she was the coolest. For some reason, I felt I needed to tell her. I knew for sure that I couldn't tell my mother—no way! So, I decided to tell my godmother. She was so surprised and shocked. She couldn't believe it. She listened to everything I had to tell her... every little detail. When I finished, she said, "You know I have to tell your mother?"

I replied, "No, why?"

She explained that it was because it was very serious, and even though I used a condom, I needed to get checked out. All I could do was beg her, "Please don't tell my mother... Please, please, Godmother, please!"

She said, "I have to Tenica because I can't take you to the doctor myself. If your mother finds out about this she would kill me, and I will never get to see you again."

My godmother and I were so close and I could talk to her about anything, but I guess not about this. She called my mother and told her to come over to her house because she needed to talk to her. Once my mother got there my godmother sat her down and told her. My mother cried! She was so upset and hurt. She didn't know what to think, do or say to me. She was more hurt than anything. She yelled and talked to me about the whole situation. She immediately called the doctor and made an appointment for me. She wanted to know who the boy was, who took me there and every other little detail about that day. At that point, she was very pissed off, and I knew I was going to be on punishment forever.

I went to see the doctor the next day. They examined me and gave me a full physical checking everything. Thank God everything came back negative and good, but the exam did show that I had sex. My mother didn't put me on any birth control because she said I was only a child. She didn't want me having sex again, and said that I better not have sex again.

I regretted that day for a very long time. At that time, I just wanted to fit in with the older crew. I was lucky I didn't get pregnant or catch any STDs. I was headed into high school, so my middle school crush went away quickly. High school was a whole other level from middle school, and the boys were different. After my experience in the 8th grade, I didn't want a boyfriend at all.

My friends had boyfriends, but not me. At the time, none of my friends knew why I didn't want a boyfriend. Nobody knew I had lost my virginity, and I didn't care to share it with anyone. I just wanted to enjoy my high school days without anyone judging me about having sex early.

Over the summer, I went to Fort Lauderdale, FL with my step sister, Autumn, and her kids. My mother started sending me a lot and I was always ready to go. Maybe this was to keep me away from the boys where we lived.

Autumn needed someone to watch the kids for her over Spring breaks and the summer, so it worked out for her too. Boy, did I have the time of my life in Fort Lauderdale. It was fun in the sun every day. The summer had gone by so fast and it was time for me to start my freshman year. I went throughout my freshman year with no boyfriend, just hanging with friends, meeting new ones and getting a feel for high school.

Freshman year came and went. Then it was summer again, and here came the sophomore year—10th grade. I was 15, slowly but surely growing into a young woman. I went into 10th grade with the same mindset I did in the 9th grade—I didn't want a boyfriend. I just wanted to do my work, hang out with my friends and clown around like I always did.

I was always the class clown for sure. If I didn't do anything else, you could always count on me for a good laugh. I don't know where it came from, but it came pretty naturally for me to act silly. My friends loved that about me. That was half of my problem in school. My teachers thought I was silly and clowning around too much.

Having sex in the 8th grade didn't advance me or make me more mature. Most kids who have sex at an early age often change. It makes them act more grown-up and sassy.

It wasn't before long that I got a boyfriend sophomore year. He was skinny, red-skinned with red hair, and he was well known because he played on the Godby High football team. His name was Zion. He was a clown and very funny, as I was.

We were totally opposite of each other in a way. A lot of girls liked him, maybe because of his red hair and cornrow braids. The football team was a plus, and his smile would brighten up anyone's day.

We would always flirt with each other in the hallway and in class. We hung out a few times. I was scared to tell my mother about him. She had become very strict since my inevitable incident in the 8th grade. I knew she wasn't going to let me date him. I started going to his football games and going over to my auntie's house. My aunt stayed in Holton Street Projects, and that's where he stayed too. He stayed right across the street from her; their buildings faced each other.

My sister Lisa and my cousin Malik knew him very well. My sister Lisa low key had a crush on his big brother, but she thought nobody knew.

Zion's dad and my mother were the same, STRICT! It was kind of hard for us to hang out if we weren't at school. I couldn't get anything past my mother. She would always ask questions and try to figure out everything. For example, she asked, "Why all of a sudden you want to go to every football game?" and "Why do you keep wanting to go to your aunt's house on the weekends?" All I could do was laugh.

My sister Lisa said, "Because she goes with Zion and he's on the football team."

Blush and smile from ear-to-ear was all that I could do. My mother was looking at me like "Really Nica." She asked,

"When is the next game because I'm going to it. I want to see who this boy is."

My eyes got big because that wasn't the response I was looking for, and I didn't know if that was a good or bad thing. I couldn't believe my mother had said that because I was expecting her to be mad or yell. She fooled me! Luckily for her, he had a game that night, so we all went to the game to watch him play football.

I couldn't stop smiling the whole night at the game. I didn't get a chance to give him a heads up that my mother was coming, so he got a surprise that night. I showed her who he was as soon as we got to the game. She actually was cheering for him. During half time I went down to let him know my mother was there and she wanted to meet him. He started smiling.

So, after the game, we went down to the locker rooms and waited for Zion to come out. When he came out, I introduced him to my mother. He was smiling and looking high strung. This was definitely a bombshell moment for us. They shook hands and asked each other, "How are you?"

With my mother's delightful smile, it seemed as if she fell in love with Zion. We chatted for a little while, then left. When we got home, she told me that he was very nice looking, sweet and very mannerable. I guess that was my okay to date him. It was official; Zion was my new boyfriend. We dated for a while and started hanging out a lot more outside of school. We would sit and talk and laugh for hours.
  Once, he came to visit me at my godmother's house and

she left to go run some errands. We just chilled and watch movies, enjoying each other. At that point, we had never kissed. The most we had done was hold hands and hug each other. But this day we decided to kiss. He kissed me and I kissed him. We both didn't want to have sex, so kissing did us just fine. I didn't know if he ever had sex before, and I didn't tell him I did before. I left it just like it was with the kissing.

We were OK with how our relationship was, and the only thing that really mattered to us was being around each other and acting silly. Playing and making each other laugh was the highlight of our relationship.

One night a group of us went to the movies because that was the new hang out spot for all the high school kids. Zion didn't come out there much on Saturdays because his daddy didn't let him. I used to miss him not being there. One night me and my best friend, Zoey, went out there to chill and met up with other friends. There were so many people from different schools and hoods. The movies and miniature golf were the places to be on Saturdays. We used to go to the stores: Rave, Body Shop, and 5-7-9 to get an outfit to wear out there. You couldn't tell us anything.

One of my best friends and I used to dress alike all the time. That was one of the things too, and boys were also doing it. Some of the boys from Rickards used to come through there in their cars with loud music, getting all the girls' attention, mine included. We didn't know who they were at first, but they were definitely older guys.
Everybody used to be in the parking lot outside of the

movies, around their cars dancing to the music and having fun. Even though I had a boyfriend, I still was having some fun. Zion didn't like that I was going out there all of the time; He wasn't feeling that at all. I was just trying to have fun with my friends.

There was one dude who drove a red car with loud music. He was such a cutie, I thought. I learned his name was Brad, and he was known by many girls. We flirted a little and exchanged numbers. You could tell he was an older guy because his demeanor was different. I still was dating Zion, but I didn't think too much of exchanging numbers. Brad and I started talking on the phone. I told Brad about Zion, but I never told Zion about Brad, and nor was I going to.

I didn't think it was cool to date both of them and neither did my friends. I don't know what made me do that, but it became crazy. I knew for a fact that my mother wasn't going to let me talk to Brad because he was two years older than I was.

As time went on, I was getting more and more attracted to Brad, which caused me to back up some from Zion. He didn't mind because he was getting a lot of fame from being on the football team. I didn't realize I really needed to choose one of them until they both got a job at the same Pet Supermarket Store.

One day, Brad called me from work to talk during his break. After we hung up the phone, I got another call from the same number. I answered it because I thought it was Brad again, but it was Zion. Oh, my Lord! That's when I find out that they were working at the same place. Of course, I didn't let them know that. I pretty much ended it with Zion and started kicking it more with Brad.

We got really close, and he was a lot more mature on so many levels. He was a ladies man too! Tallahassee is so small, so I guess it was easy to be one. We started off just dating and then got into a relationship quickly.

I started skipping school and lying to my mother that I was staying at a friend's house just so I could be with him. I had it bad. Everywhere Brad and his friends went, I tried to be in that same place. I always had my best friend Zoey or another close friend with me. They both were talking to one of his friends, so it made it easier for me to hang with them all at once.

My mother didn't approve of Brad at all, but my stepdad was a little cooler. He pulled Brad to the side and talked to him a couple of times and laid down some laws. My mother still didn't like the fact that we were talking. She had a night job, so my stepdad would let him come over and chill with me.

Things got real serious between us, and I ended up pregnant from him. I wasn't too shocked because I knew the first time we had sex without a condom, I was going to get pregnant and I was right! My mother must've felt it because one day I put on some shorts and my mother replied, "Tenica, you look like you gaining weight. Are you pregnant?"
I looked at her and said, "No, I am not."

I was in the 10th grade and he was in the 12th. When I found out I was pregnant, I didn't know who in the hell was going to tell my mother because it wasn't going to be me! I tried to get my best friend to tell her for me, but that didn't work out so well.

So I did it myself, and I had my best friend Zoey right by my side. I sat my mother down and told her I needed to tell her something. I told her I was pregnant. Her response was, "OK, so what are you going to do about it?"

I looked at her and said, "I want to keep it."

She said, "OK," and got up from the table. So, Zoey and I looked at each other, smiled and got up too. My stepdad Joe didn't really approve of the news, but he wasn't really mad. I knew they had my back no matter what happened.

Then, I went to tell my biological dad, Jerry. I was nauseous to tell him, but I told him. He was so mad he pulled out a gun on me and was going off. I was crying and called my mother. He was over the top about this pregnancy, and I couldn't understand why because he didn't really do much for me anyway, as far as actually taking care of me. My mother did everything for me and always took care of me, especially financially. I was so upset, but my mother told me not to even worry about it, and she called him and went right back off on him. I left his house and I didn't talk to him for a while. When I was little I was kind of a daddy's girl until I got into my teenage stage. I couldn't think about my dad because it wasn't about him.

At that moment, my life was about to change because I was

bringing a child in the world, and I wasn't ready. I wasn't prepared, but I didn't have a choice, but to be ready. As soon as I found out that I was about 2 months in my pregnancy, I went looking for a place to stay. I applied for every program I could think of that helped teen moms. Any assistance I could get, I applied for it. My mother wasn't too happy about that because she felt I was moving too fast, but I didn't want to waste time, I wanted to have my own place for my baby and I.

As I got farther along in my pregnancy, it wasn't bad at all. It actually was an easy pregnancy. I was a little ashamed though because I was only 17 and still in high school. I didn't want all my other friends' mothers to think differently of me, and I didn't want to lose my friends because of it. But things turned out totally differently, and my friends and their mothers were very supportive of me. My pregnancy was easier because I had a great support system behind me throughout it.

My mother had my back and my front, and teen mothers need that. She begged me not to move out just yet. Since I was a first-time mom, she wanted me to wait at least a year after the baby was born. So, I stayed with her, and she was right about that. I appreciated everyone because I was a first-time mom. Brad was there throughout the pregnancy. His mother wasn't too happy about it. She didn't even believe that the baby was his, and she requested a paternity test to be done. I didn't give her one because Brad knew it was his child, and her thoughts and opinions didn't even matter to me. Either she was going to be in my child's life or not.

We both were still in school. He was a senior and his prom

came up so he asked me to go with him to Rickards High School prom. At first, I was like heck no because I was pregnant. But my mother and friends talked me into going. My mother got me a dress and got my hair and makeup done. I had the time of my life. And to be honest, I went to Godby High and Rickards High proms. We all had a ball. I'm glad I didn't miss that opportunity.

The day that we found out what we were having, he went to the doctor's office with me. When they announced that it was a boy, he was super happy. It was from that point on that things really began to get real in my life.

My mother and friends threw me one of the best baby showers ever. I was overwhelmed with so much love, joy, gifts, friends, and family. One of Brad's closest friends was there with me throughout the whole pregnancy as well. He never left my side—you would've thought that he was my baby daddy. Some people thought that though, seriously! His name was Jared, and I appreciated him for keeping in touch so much, even if Brad wasn't there.

As it got closer to the delivery, things started changing with Brad and I. We started having problems with chicks he was cheating on me with. He started dating multiple girls. I wasn't able to get out and move around like I used to. He was young too, and he definitely wasn't ready to be a teen parent. I had already made my decision that I was keeping the baby and my pregnancy was nearly over.

I tried not to focus on the stuff he was doing because I didn't want to harm the baby in any kind of way. My 18th birthday came and I felt a little bad that I couldn't celebrate it like I wanted to because I was pregnant. My friend Natalie came and got me out of the house to celebrate so that I wouldn't feel so pregnant, which was hard to do because I was ready to pop.

Things were getting crazy for me with the pregnancy going to school. I had my mother to withdraw me from Godby High School and enroll me into Lively Tap School for Pregnant Girls. That was best for me, and I was able to work at my own pace. I ended the school year there in 12th grade with a completion. I didn't receive my diploma, and I didn't walk across the stage. I was sad about that, but it was getting closer and closer to my due date so I stopped going to school.

It wasn't long before my baby boy was here. He was born on June 14th, 2000, and that was one of the best days of my life. I cried so much when I held him in my arms for the first time. I had all my close friends there, and of course my mother, big sister Sasha and godmother. His dad was there too.

I didn't know at the moment I was about to become a single parent. His daddy wasn't coming around as much. I don't know if it was because of his mother or not. She wasn't feeling any of the baby stuff. And she wanted to be in control over everything. But my mother said, "No way!"
Eventually, his mother started coming around some and started doing stuff for our baby boy. Things were going pretty well for the baby and I. My sister Lisa wasn't there throughout my pregnancy because she went to Job Corps and then to the Navy! But, when she got the news Romelo

was born, she came home.

I really had no worries because she had him stuck to her like glue! She was so in love with him. That was her baby from day one. Luckily, because I needed all the help I could get. My dad even got over whatever he had going on about me being pregnant. He even babysat sometimes when I needed him too. I guess he was just being a concerned parent when he first found out. He could've handled it differently but it was no love lost from us.

Romelo's dad had up and moved to Tampa, Florida. It was Romelo's first birthday and his dad had moved. It was a bit of a shocker, but I wasn't surprised at all. Things changed after I had the baby, and you could tell he didn't want the responsibility once the baby was actually here. Unfortunately, his mother didn't force or make him step up to be the father he should've been because things didn't go her way. Nothing seemed consistent with them. But that wasn't going to stop me from doing what I had to do and do for my baby boy.

I grew up really fast and became a mother before any of my friends. Motherhood welcomed me with open arms and lots of challenges.

Tenica Cofield

CHAPTER 4
CHALLENGES OF LIFE

Stress and depression have played a big role in my life. My first time experiencing stress or depression was in 2001. I was a first-time mom working my first real job and had just moved out into my own place.

I had applied for Section 8 (low-income housing) when I first found out I was pregnant because I didn't want to stay with my mother or put a burden on her. Everything I could apply for I did, including food stamps, Medicaid, and Early Childhood Coalition. These were benefits given out by the government, so I applied for them all.

My son's dad wasn't a part of his life, so I had to do everything on my own starting at the age of 19. My mother helped as much as she could. But, stress and depression can sneak up on you and you wouldn't even know that you're stressing.

There was so much going on in my life when I was 19 years old. I had so much on my plate and it was like there wasn't no breakthrough. I was doing my best to be a young mom and take care of my son by myself, on top of still having a social life with my friends.

When you have a child you're responsible for someone else's

life, not only yours anymore. But, I wanted to continue to club and party like my friends were. At times, I questioned why I had to get pregnant so early. It seemed as if I couldn't move like I wanted to and I was growing up so much faster than I wanted to. I started losing a large amount of weight, not having an appetite. Paying bills, staying home all the time, going to work, taking and picking up my child from daycare, and taking care of him by myself—I was beyond submerged.

I didn't realize how much weight I was losing until my mother and friends starting saying, "Tenica, you're getting so skinny. Why are you losing weight? What's wrong with you?"

They questioned me each time they saw me. Typically, I would say, "Nothings wrong with me, I'm fine."

There were nights I would sit up all night just looking at my baby boy. I couldn't go to sleep even when I tried to! At that time, I had to be at work by 5:30 am. I used to ask myself what's going on, what's wrong with me. I began questioning myself as my mother and friends did.

My income wasn't enough at Leon County School Board Transportation. People think just because you're on Section 8 that your bills don't amount to anything. Perhaps that's the case for some people, but definitely not for all. The more or little you make, everything goes up... not to mention the things that government assistance doesn't cover. There were so many times that I didn't have enough to pay all of my bills, especially daycare. I was getting so tired of that.

I felt that I was so skinny at that point and that I looked so ugly compared to my friends and other women. I was 20 years old with a baby and his dad left and moved to Tampa, Florida. My son was only one year old. How could someone just up and leave their firstborn like that?

I found myself worrying about things I shouldn't have been worrying about. When I moved out on my own, everything was good and I thought I was making the best decision. But, all of a sudden everything hit me so fast transitioning into real adulthood. Overwhelmed became a natural state for me; it's as if I just started letting it have its way. It was a heavy load for a person. A lot of people said, "Oh this what happens when you think you're grown and have sex or have a baby!"

Everything had gotten so bad that I stopped going to work. The easy situation I thought I had, had turned into something so difficult. I would stay in bed all day. I had so many "No Call, No Shows" on my record at work. My mother had no idea that I was missing work like that or that I was going through a depression like that.

I would miss work one day without calling and just show up the next day like it wasn't a problem at all. I didn't care if the supervisor knew or not or what she would do to me. I seriously did this so much, and not just for days or weeks. I did this for months, just not showing up to work or calling. Sometimes, if I didn't want to do a "No Call, No Show" I would call off from work because I didn't have the energy to go. I felt so tired all of the time. I would just lay in bed all day by myself. I would take my son to daycare, then go back home and get in bed until it was time to pick him up.

I didn't have any boyfriends or guy friends that I was hanging with or seeing. I didn't want any and I was just so stressed out, not eating and having terrible migraines. I called my child's dad for help and he claimed that he didn't have it. I was so angry because my son didn't ask to be brought into this world. I felt that he was a blessing to us both and I shouldn't be stressing and depressed trying to take care of him alone.

He was in Tampa living a carefree life with no worries, no stress, and no depression! Sometimes his mother would try to help out with some things, but it wasn't enough, and he pretty much wouldn't do anything. I think the most he ever did was pay for asthma medication for our son. I got tired of calling trying to get help from him. I put him on Child Support but he was half paying that too.

I had only been on my own maybe less than two years. One Sunday, I decided to go to church with my mother, stepsister Maya, stepdad and son. I wasn't really feeling well that morning or the whole weekend. Of course, I had barely eaten anything all weekend. I didn't even have the energy to stand or walk, but I made my way to church. My vision was so indistinct, my head was hurting exceedingly bad and I knew it had to be a migraine.

I was starting to have them more often than usual. But I knew I had to be in church, and I wanted to be with my mother. As I entered to go sit in the church I was okay enough. I didn't really feel like myself, but I hadn't been myself lately, so that had become a normal feeling for me at that time. The pastor began preaching his usual sermon and the more he talked, the more dizzy and light-headed I felt. I told my mother to watch my son, and I walked to the bathroom and put water on my face.

It was getting scarier than usual when I'm at home. I felt like I couldn't walk, so I just sat in the bathroom for a couple minutes trying to get myself together. I was thinking one thing and my body was doing another. We were not on the same page at all. I wasn't sure if it was because I hadn't eaten all weekend or what, but it was starting to scare me. I took a deep breath and walked back in the sanctuary with my mother and everyone else.

I sat down next to my son and continued to listen to the pastor's word. Then came the dizziness and a bad headache, which I knew was about to turn into a migraine. I was trying so hard not to distract my mother or let anybody know what was going on. It is hard to remain calm when your body is feeling like it's about to shut down on you.

During the service, the pastor asked everyone to stand up for prayer. I gathered my son and we stood up. As I was standing, my body began to feel more and weaker. I thought to myself, Lord, what's happening to me? I touched my mother who was standing next to me and told her, "I don't feel good! I feel so dizzy and light-headed."

She told me to go drink some water. So I sat my son down, went to the bathroom again and drank some water from the water fountain. I stood there for a minute but wasn't feeling any better at all. I walked back in and told my mother that

I felt so light-headed and I had a huge migraine. Next thing I know, I fainted in church with my son in my arms. I woke up with my mother, stepdad and Stepsister Maya, standing around me asking, "Nica, Are you OK?"

Then, I heard my mother say, "Let's take her to the hospital right now!"

So we got up and walked out of the church. Maya was holding my son and my mother was holding and helping me walk while my stepdad got the car. I felt everybody in the church was looking at me. I felt so ashamed but it really didn't matter because I thought I was dying. I couldn't feel anything and could barely see because my vision was so blurry. So off to the hospital we went.

I just laid back in the seat, looking up at the sky. I wasn't thinking or anything, just looking out the window into the sky. My family was talking to me and saying stuff, but to be honest, everything was just noise. I was literally zoned out. When we arrived at the hospital, they rushed me into the emergency room. As we waited in the waiting room, nothing had changed with me at all. I was still very weak, had a migraine, very light-headed with blurry vision, and I had begun to feel nauseous.

They called me in triage. First, she had me get on the scale to check my weight. Lord Jesus, I was 125 pounds. My mother said, "Oh my God, Nica!"

I said to my mother, "I guess this explains why I'm down to double zero sized clothes now!"

After she wrote my weight down, she asked us some questions to see what was going on with me. We informed the nurse of all the symptoms I was having, and then I went on to tell the nurse that I hadn't been eating. She looked, And said, "Oh you haven't eaten today?"

I said, "No, I haven't been eating at all. I've been going days and nights without eating or drinking, and I have been doing this for a few months. Also, I've been having numerous thoughts of suicide."

The nurse looked at me and then my mother was looking at me. The look in my mother's eyes was sorrowful and startled. I put my head down for a second because I couldn't look at my mother in her eyes. Her eyes got so watery. The nurse continued to check me in at triage but didn't ask any more questions at that time. After she took my blood pressure and pulse, she directed us back out to the sitting room with my stepdad, stepsister and son.

He was sleeping peacefully, and I was glad of that. I didn't want him seeing me like that even though he had no idea what was going on. My stepdad, Joe, asked my mother what was going on what did they say. My mother looked at him as if she didn't want to repeat what she had just heard in there. She began to tell him, "Tenica hasn't been eating and she's been having suicidal thoughts."

My step dad said, "What?"

Tears were falling down my face. I couldn't stop crying, and my mother's eyes were just as bad as mine. She didn't say too much to me as we waited in the waiting room. She just looked at me. The emergency room was pretty full that day. They didn't have a room for me, but they put me in a bed and we had to wait in the hallway. As I laid in bed I was just shaking, shaking, and shaking. We had to ask the nurse to give me some blankets.

The doctor finally came out to see what was going on. And I told him the same thing I told the nurse. I hadn't been eating or able to eat in the past couple of months. I had just been so tired, without energy, and I'd also been having bad migraines. He asked me, "Are you stressed or depressed?"

I said to him, "I'm not sure what's going on with me. This really is my first time going through something like this. I thought it was stress but I wasn't about to put a name on it. I'm a first-time mom, and it's just me and my son who stays together."

So he told us, "I'll tell you what! We're going to run some tests on you to see what is going on."

They began to run tests on me. In the meantime, my mother was praying over me. I knew she was at a lost for words and couldn't believe what was going on. Me either, to be real! Finally, the tests came back and the doctor said that my tests showed that I'm stressed. He had run a stress test on me. Another one of the tests showed that I was very dehydrated, so the doctor told them to give me an IV to put some fluids in my body.
He told me that my migraines were coming from all the

stressing that I had been doing. He explained how that wasn't healthy at all for me. I could have a stroke or heart attack. I was too young to be doing all that stressing, especially with my baby. Staying alone with nobody else there with us was not helping. I felt so bad but I couldn't help it. Things were hard for me.

The doctor told me if I didn't start eating that I would have to come back and if I did that they would have to put a feeding tube inside of me, and he knew I didn't want that. I promised him and my mother that I was going to start eating and doing better, but I wasn't sure if I really meant that because I still had so much stuff stressing me out. I couldn't sit there and tell him differently though because I was ready to go, my mother and the rest of them were looking at me, and I was afraid that they would admit me into the hospital.

I wasn't trying to stay there any longer than I had to. So I agreed to everything. He also prescribed me some medication for stress, depression and to help me have an appetite to eat. I got discharged from the hospital. My mother then took me home, and of course, she tried to talk to me, but I just told her I was stressing over my bills and trying to take care of my son. I really wanted to tell her about the many suicidal thoughts, but I didn't.

I stayed off of Mission Road in the Stratford Landing Apartments. Whenever I came around that corner off White Drive, I saw a big tree there. I would have thoughts of just running my car into that tree. Millions of times those thoughts crossed my mind, but I would just keep going. On many occasions, I would lock myself in my bathroom with a knife and put the knife to my wrist as if I'm about to cut it. But I never did, I'd just get on the bathroom floor and cry. I wanted to tell my mother these things, but I decided not to.

As the days went by, I was taking my medicine and trying to do better. My three best friends had no idea what was going on. Eventually, I ended up telling one of them because me and her were closer than the others. I also told my friend Larry who was like a brother to me. I needed someone to talk to. When I told them what happened on Sunday, neither one of them could believe it. Larry said that's why I was so skinny. They felt so sorry for me! So, they both agreed that it's a lot that I'm doing by myself and it wasn't fair. They decided to stay the night with me to keep me and my son company. I appreciated that because I was lonely and I was trying my best to be better and do better as the doctor ordered.

More time went by and I was getting up going to work, eating, taking care of my son as always, and gaining some of the weight back. If the medicine wasn't doing anything else it was definitely putting weight on me. I did notice that I was starting to smile more and trying to manage things differently. My mother and step dad continued to help out as much as they could. They even offered for me to move back home. I told them no, I'm going to get through this and I'm going to be OK.

I was starting to feel so much better and was taking my medicine regularly. It became the norm for me, like taking vitamins. But the doctor told me after a couple of months, maybe three months, I could stop taking them. I knew that all of this was a big scare for me and I didn't want to hurt myself or hurt my mother anymore. More importantly, my son needs me.

Sometimes we have no control over our thoughts. At least that's what I felt. I know I didn't want to be on that medication long like the doctor said, so getting it together was the plan at that time.

Tenica Cofield

CHAPTER 5
UNTOLD SECRET

Nightmares are the scariest thing anyone could have. The thing about nightmares is not knowing if they are real or not. I never really had nightmares as a child, that I could remember at least. Once I was between the ages of 20 and 25 years old, I started having these bad dreams, like every night on and off and over and over. I mean they were coming more often than ever and I didn't know why. I use to think to myself, Mmmm, am I too old to be having nightmares?

In my mind, I would be lying down asleep in my bed and my room door would be open. My heart would start beating and racing so fast. It was beginning to be very frightening. I could not figure out what was going on with me and these nightmares. I was having these nightmares frequently and it was like someone was trying to tell me something in my dream.

Well, I certainly wouldn't call them dreams because they were scary. I don't know if someone was trying to show me something or what. This was the creepiest thing ever. I didn't know what to do, think or who to tell about my nightmares. There wasn't much to it but me in my room lying in bed and the door was open, but the scenery in the nightmare was horrible.

This really had me feeling mentally deranged. I knew if I told anyone they would quickly think I'm crazy. It got to the point where I didn't want to go back to sleep at night. I would try to stay awake all night if I could. I recall one night after the club, I came home and was sitting up because I was too anxious to go to sleep, but I dozed off because I was sleepy and was tipsy from the club. Here comes this nightmare again with me lying in the bed in my room.

I could see that I was a little girl. Well, that's what it felt like at least. The door opened, and this time, I acknowledged the existence of the room. Someone walked in the room, but I couldn't discern their face. I woke up out of the nightmare, tossing and turning throughout the rest of the night. I tossed and turned so much that night I really couldn't go back to sleep.

It was becoming very difficult, and I couldn't make out what was going on. It was the very same thing every night, but it seemed as if something was different and weird about each one of the nightmares. Why was this happening to me?

I wanted to share with someone because I thought maybe they would help me to understand. I felt like I needed some help because I knew this wasn't normal. I wasn't on drugs, well I did smoke weed but I didn't think that was the problem. There really wasn't much to tell anyone anyway because I didn't have all the answers myself.

There seemed to be no way out of these fearsome night-mares. I even tried putting my son in the bed with me because I thought that would help in some kind of way. I was trying to figure out solutions and see what this nightmare was about. I didn't recall watching any horror movies related to the dreams I was having at night. Man, I thought I was going crazy and losing my mind, so I knew if I told somebody else they would think the same.

I didn't believe myself and I was starting to be afraid of myself. It was so unexplainable. I was losing so much sleep it was ridiculous! I told myself that I was going to fight this and it was not going to take over my sleep.

One night, I went to sleep and here comes this bad nightmare again but I woke up. But that's not what I wanted to do. I needed to go back to sleep so I could surface the dream again to see what was going on or who was trying to tell me something. That's what came to mind, that maybe someone was trying to tell me something and I wasn't listening. I was getting pissed because I was sick of this and I was missing so much sleep. This needs to end right away, I thought to myself a thousand times.

Not getting the bona fide rest I needed was becoming very unnerving. I felt I had to tell my mother or at least go see a doctor about my issue. My mother and stepdad counseled people who were on drugs, so I figured they could help me. I needed help as soon as possible or I was going to lose it. I couldn't keep going to work or about my day with no rest.

I just wasn't feeling like myself. People didn't know though, as usual, especially my friends. I prayed to God, asking him to not allow me to have another nightmare and whatever this

63

is, please just let it go away. I didn't know if God heard my prayer or not. I was hoping that my prayer was good enough that I shouldn't have any more problems going to sleep. It was funny because I only had problems at night when I went to sleep, but never when I took a nap. I thought that was very strange.

After a long day at work, I cooked, showered and got me and my baby to bed as usual. I didn't even think about what was going to happen when I tried to go to sleep. I just fell asleep. The nightmare came. I was in my room lying down in my bed. My room door opens and this tall boy walks in. I jumped up out of bed and he pushed me back down on the bed and then proceeded to climb on top of me. He would lay on top of me, moving himself up and down with his private part on my private part. I didn't know who the person was or exactly what he was doing to me.

He never took my clothes off or down; he was just repeating the same thing over and over again. I was just lying there with my eyes closed. I would open my eyes, look at him quickly, and shut my eyes again, praying and hoping he would get off me, waiting for my mommy to come home.

Then, I woke up out of my sleep screaming and crying. I even woke my baby up because I was screaming so loud. I was sweating profusely. My pillow was covered with sweat. When I sat up in my bed looking around the room thinking to myself, Oh my God, I recognized the room and the face. It was my room from when we stayed in the Macon neighborhood. All I could think was What the hell?
It was coming to me, and it felt like it was a movie. I realized

what was going on. It was my oldest brother, Jason. WOW! Believe it or not, I was going into a shock about to really lose my mind! Jason had been molesting me when I was a little girl when we lived in Macon neighborhood, and this was happening on various occasions.

Everything was coming to me as clear as day. It's like the vision of those days were showing up in my mind. And all I could do was replay what was done to me when I was little. This was unbelievable! He would come into the room when I was asleep and nobody was at the house. He would get on top of me all the time and put his private part on mine and move up and down. I couldn't see or remember for how long he was doing it.

Jason and I didn't grow up in the same house together, but I do remember him and Sasha used to come over to our house when we lived in Macon. I think they even stayed with us for a while over there. I couldn't accept the fact that my oldest brother Jason had molested me as a little child. I had to at least be around five or six years old. Yes, I was an innocent little girl who was harmless and unable to defend herself. I was still nearly a baby.

With this recovered memory, I sat in the house for days wondering how I was going to tell my mother about this nightmare that was actually a real-life event. How was I going to tell my mother what her son did to her baby girl? This hurt me so bad because we're both her children and that's my brother. I didn't want to have these nightmares or visions. I was hoping after the fact that it wasn't true and it was all just a crazy nightmare. But all I could think about was

"Where was my mother when this was going on?"

My friends and mother were calling during these days of devastation, but I was barely talking to them. I didn't want anybody to know. I had so many thoughts and unanswered questions tormenting my brain. Trying to figure all of it out was making it worse for me. It even crossed my mind where were my other siblings when that was going on? And did this happen when my mother was at work? I just didn't get it, no matter how hard I tried.

It made me think about the times we were around each other when we were older. It seemed like he just couldn't look me in my eyes, I swear! I used to wonder why he acted weird around me or why he seemed so nervous when we were in each other's presence. When he came around, I noticed he acted so weird or seemed mortified to look at me. Our relationship has been mysterious. It seemed like we weren't even sister and brother, but I thought it came from us not really growing up with each other.

There were times I told my mother that he acted oddly when he came around me now that we're adults. This was way before I even came to grips with these unpleasant nightmares. The more I thought about it, the more sickened I became of it. At the time the abuse happened, my brother was at least 15 or 16 years of age. He was somewhat a kid himself, but this didn't give him the right to do this to his baby sister or any other child. As I thought about the situation and tried to put the pieces together, I was curious to know if he even remembered. After a couple of days went by, I didn't want to be around him anymore, and I hadn't talked to a soul about it, but he was on my mind. The thought of it had my stomach and whole body all messed up. I didn't feel the same anymore! And I felt so ashamed of something I didn't have control over. Everything about it freaked me out. I didn't want to deal with any of my siblings anymore.

My heart was broken, and I thought if I shared it, no one would believe me or understand what this feeling was like. I didn't even think that anyone would take this matter seriously or if he would care that I understood what he did to me when I was a little girl. I would have so many moments where I would just break down and cry. It felt like a part of me was taken from me without my permission.

To me, it didn't matter if my clothes were up or down; he did something that shouldn't have been done. This was wearing me down, and I had to tell my mother. I had to call her right away. As I dialed her number, I started crying. When she picked up the phone, I said, "Ma."

She replied, "What's wrong with you?"

She could hear the shriek in my voice. I said to her, "I've been having some bad dreams or nightmares and I couldn't sleep at night."

She said, "OK, and?"

Then I said to her, "I couldn't understand my nightmares at first or figure them out but now I do. Jason used to molest me when we stayed in the Macon Neighborhood Apartments." My mother got noiseless on the phone. It was like she wasn't even on the phone anymore. As I was I talking I continued to cry because I can often be dramatic when something is wrong. I began to describe to her about the terrifying nightmares. Then I heard her breathe, so I knew she was still there. "Ma," I said to her, "In my nightmare, I would be laying down in the bed and the door would open. At first, that's all I was seeing, but the more nights I had nightmares, and the longer I would stay asleep, they would come in more detail.

Jason would come in my room while I was in bed and lay down on top of me. He would put his private part on my private part and press his body on me while moving up and down. Sometimes he would put his hands in places that were inappropriate. Why did he put his private part more between my legs?"

The tears were just rolling as I told all this to my mother. Then, I started to say, "I know you don't believe me and you think I'm making this all up because you're not saying anything. But I'm not lying! This is true and this happened to me."

And then my mother said to me, "Nica, baby, no, I believe you. You're not lying, and I believe everything you're saying. I believe he did that to you because somebody close to him did the exact same thing to someone else."

Disturbance is all I felt when those words came out of my mother's mouth. She told me, "Stop crying, it's going to be OK. I know it probably hurt and you feel scared, lost and confused, but it's OK."
I replied, "No, Ma, it's not OK. That's not right!"

She said, "It's not right, but what's done is done. I'm sorry that happened to you. My advice to you is that you sit him down and talk to him about it or just let it go. I love you and there's nothing we can do, but pray and ask God to help you forgive him and give you healing from this."

All I said to her was, "Alright," and got off the phone with her.

I sat and thought about it and prayed. I knew if I talked to him about it that he was going to deny it and say it wasn't true, as if I was crazy or delusional. His wife was going to say I made up the whole thing up because that's her husband now. I could be wrong, but I don't feel I would get any answers from talking to him. Even though my mother knew I was telling the truth, I couldn't expect everyone else to believe me.

This was just going to blow up into a big mess. I just wished it never happened to me, period. I decided to let it go and keep it to myself, my mother and God. I still think about it all of the time. Sometimes I'm afraid to be alone because I think somebody is going to come in my room.

No-one knows my untold secret that I'm scared to sleep by myself to this day. I try to socialize with my brother when I see him. It's hard for me. That was more than 25 years ago when this happened to me.

I know this has been done to many girls and boys. They're afraid to let anyone know or feel ashamed of it. They may even feel that it didn't happen. But, it did. God has a way of disclosing and showing us things that happened in our lives or things we need to know. I don't know God's reason for revealing it to me, but I know it's a good reason. I will no longer question it, but I'm glad I know it. I don't think I'll ever forget, but I'm working on forgiving him without him even knowing.

CHAPTER 6
SWEET VS SOUR

Well, like most girls, there were three guys who I went to school with that we referred to one another as sister and brother. Larry, Levi, and Cameron were my "brothers." I met those guys at Griffin Middle and Godby High School.

Cameron used to stay across the street from me when I stayed with my mother, and Levi used to be one of my neighbors on the North side of town. Levi had the biggest crush on me and everybody knew it.

At that age, I was the only one out of my friends to have their own spot. My house was the true hangout spot for everyone to come over and chill. Levi made sure he was on every scene that I was because he was so crazy about Tenica. We were already cool from school and like brothers and sisters, but eventually, we started to utilize our texting to flirt some.

Levi shared a spot with his cousin. Their apartment pretty much became a hangout spot for me and my best friend Zoey. Levi's cousin had a crush on Zoey, so that worked out perfect for Levi and me to meet up and chill without the entire crew.

Levi used to pick on me all the time when I was pregnant

and said that it should've been his baby. He was cool with my son and was around him a lot just like the rest of my homeboys. Of course, baby Romelo was the crew's baby, so everybody said.

Larry was dating my cousin Nicole at the time. She and I were like cool cousins since we were little girls. Nicole was about two years older than me, but that didn't make a difference to us. We used to fuss and fight, but we were still close. Even though I stayed on the North side of town and Nicole was still staying on the South side, we still hung out all of the time.

There were plenty of times where Nicole, Levi, his cousin and I would hang out at their house. There were also times where Zoey, Levi, his cousin and I hung out too. Some kind of way Levi and I would end up chilling together, drinking, smoking and watching movies. I guess you could say that Levi and I were dating because we weren't in a relationship but we were chilling at each other's houses and had sex a couple of times.

See, I really looked at Levi as the annoying friend, which he knew and everyone else did too. I would always crack jokes on him, but we were so close and cool. I literally kept everyone laughing making fun of him. I really didn't take what we were doing that serious, but he did. Our dating relationship didn't last long at all but it didn't change the friendship.

Larry and Nicole didn't last long, and Zoey and Levi's cousin didn't either. We were all just trying something I guess because we were mostly friends, hangout crew, and super cool with each other.

Every time we got together, everybody would bring up me and Levi dating because he still liked me in that way. Larry wasn't in a relationship with my cousin Nicole anymore, but we all would still hang. He was also my sons god daddy. Larry was the ladies man. It wasn't before long that Larry started dating again.

Soon after, he started dating Chloe. She was one of my best friends and Romelo's godsister. We all hung out together. Chloe and Larry were dating and had more than what he had, with Nicole. Him and Chloe were together all the time and everywhere together. My relationship didn't change with Larry. We were still close and hanging like siblings. I thought it was cool for them to date because they were a great fit for one another. I cared for both of them and we all were like a big friend-family.

He treated her so nicely. Whatever she needed, he made sure she was straight. She didn't have to ask much from him.

There were times when we would go out to the Moon night club and Larry would come through with his homeboys. Chloe would be smiling from ear to ear, and Larry would be smiling back at her the same. He was a dope boy, street dude, and they were definitely popping at that time. Larry had a mouth full of gold teeth with the dreads. He was so sweet though because he always looked out for everyone.

Sometimes, I was like a middle man in their relationship

because I was so close to both of them. Whenever they had problems with one another or got mad at each other, they both would come to me. I would try to mediate the situation. Chloe would call and tell me to talk to my brother or see if my brother Larry was mad. You know how friends did back then and around that age.

Your homegirls will talk to your boyfriend for you when you're mad at each other. I was cool with that because my friendship with Larry meant a lot. Our bond was so tight like brothers and sisters. Whenever I said Romelo needed something, Larry would make sure he got it. He was always doing for Romelo, especially since his dad wasn't in the picture. That made me and Larry close. He spent so much time over at my house checking up on me and Romelo.

At first, Romelo didn't like Larry at all. He would run from him every time he came over to visit, and he would cry. But one day Larry pulled out a twenty-dollar bill and told Romelo to come get it, and surprisingly, he ran to him. It was too funny! Ever since that day, Romelo hasn't been scared of him.

Larry was always playing with Romelo and showing him so much love. I appreciated him for that. People always thought that Larry and I were messing around with each other, but it wasn't like that. We really had a genuine friendship. I always looked at him as a street boy with a lot of females because I watched how he did things.

Nobody ever knew, but I would always get on Larry about his lifestyle and all of those girls. I knew exactly what kind of dude he was, and he was not in my favorite category. Larry and I were opposite of each other. Actually, I was opposite from most of my friends. I had a shyness about me when it came to dudes, especially after my firstborn child.

I wasn't too happy about my body. I was always the skinny one out of the group. My other three homegirls were thick, with hips and booty. I was skinny with big teeth in my mouth. Dudes were attracted to me still, a lot of them. But I wouldn't give them the time of day. I wasn't happy with how I looked before and after High school.

My homegirls had a few friends and weren't afraid to talk to dudes. They weren't out there like that with a lot of guys but they weren't scared to talk to any either. They kept it classy, cute and on the low because no one would ever know who they were talking too. They used to tell me, "Tenica, you need to loosen up and get you a dude." It was about my son, not other men, in my eyes.

One day, Larry asked if he could move in with me because of his living situation with his grandmother. I let him move in because we were cool. That was my brother, so I let him stay. Larry was able to come and go as he pleased, there was no pressure at all. His family really thought we were messing around when I let him move in with me. But there was nothing between us, and he was barely even at the house.

My homegirls would still come over and chill with us. By that time, him and Chloe had broken up, but everybody was still cool as usual. His crew and my crew of friends continued to do our normal thing on the weekends.

One time, Larry had gotten in some trouble and had to do some community service hours. He needed a ride home one night, so I asked my best friend Zoey to take me to pick him up. We went and on the way back to my house, Larry kept rubbing on my shoulder. I thought, "What in the hell," but I didn't know what he had going on. Zoey had no idea what was going on in the car.

Once we got to my house and Larry got out of the car, I told her what he was doing. She was laughing and saying, "Hell No."

She could believe it though because Larry tried to talk to her before, and she gave him a little conversation, but not much because she wasn't feeling him like that at all. I didn't think too much of any of it because I knew I wasn't going to talk to Larry like that. After all, I knew everything about his butt and how he rolled. Things did seem a little weird though after that night.

Larry was still staying with me, so we had to see each other. I just continued to act normal and he did the same from that day forward. My cousin came over to stay the weekend with me, and I let her sleep on one of the sofas. Romelo and I had fallen asleep on the other sofa where Larry usually slept, but he was hanging out that night so I wasn't sure if he was coming to the house afterward.

There was a knock on the door at around midnight. It was Larry. He said it was freezing out so he came in early. I told him my cousin was there and we're sleeping on the sofa, so he could just sleep in my bed. He said that he would sleep on the floor. I told him no, just get in my bed since I was already sleeping in the living room. I went and got back on the sofa, which began to get very uncomfortable after a while, so I went to get in my bed. I didn't mind that Larry was in there.

He was on one side, knocked out, and I got on the other side. It was no big deal. We had lived with each other for about two months at that point and we saw each other get dressed all of the time. I got in bed and went to sleep. Larry was sleeping so hard, I figured he had no clue that I was even in the bed with him. We were sleeping well, at least that's what I thought until I felt Larry's hand rubbing on my body. I thought I was dreaming at first. I woke up and realized this was really happening. I knew what was about to go down and I didn't stop it. He started kissing on me, and one thing led to another, and of course, we had sex.

When I woke up the next day, I was confused. What had just happened? I actually didn't feel too good about it. And I let him know that. My body felt so bizarre all over. It felt good for that moment, but it didn't the next day. It literally made me sick to my stomach. I couldn't even look at him that day, the next day and any day after that. Throughout the whole day, I was barely talking to him. However, he was fine with what happened the night before. It didn't bother him at all. And that next day of all days, he stayed in the house mostly.

He had finally got dressed and left the house. I got up and took a shower, still trying to figure out what just happened. Having sex with Larry was a huge mistake. I had to think of a way to get him to move out. After that happened, I knew he couldn't continue to stay with me. It was bothering me too much. It was crazy how it was on my mind. I had to call my best friend Zoey to let her know what happened that night. She couldn't believe that we had slept together either.

I told her I had to think of something to tell him to get him out of my house. But, I didn't want it to mess up our friendship. I waited a couple of days to decide what to say to him. I went to work with it on my mind; it was just that serious to me. At the time, I hadn't told anybody but my best friend Zoey. Before anyone else could find out, I knew I had to deal with the situation.

So, I called him and told him we needed to talk after I got off work. When I got home from work I told him that my landlord did an inspection at the apartment. She saw his clothes in Romelo's closet and said he had to move because I couldn't have anybody staying with me. Of course, it was a lie, but I couldn't think of anything else to say. Larry was okay with it and said, "No problem," and took his stuff and moved out that day.

It was a relief but I felt bad. I thought about my close friend Chloe and my cousin Nicole. I thought everything would be better since he moved out, but he kept calling. I told him to stop calling me but he didn't stop at all. Days went by and he showed up at my house. I had to prepare myself before I opened the door because I was serious about us not messing around with each other. As soon as I opened the door, Larry was so delighted to see me, and the compassion wasn't reciprocated.

I asked him what was he doing at my house. I told him not to call me or come back over to the house. Larry said, "I know but I came to see Romelo and you to make sure y'all were okay." I let him visit for a while, then he left. He tried to give me a kiss and hug but I wouldn't let him. I told him that we couldn't do this because he used to date Chloe and Nicole and it wasn't right. On top of the fact that Levi used to like me and we messed around. He looked at me and said, "Just know, what I want I get." And he was right! All the avoiding I tried to do with him didn't work at all, not answering calls, texts! He didn't care and he wouldn't stop. He told me I need to stop playing hard to get, but I didn't want to mess up our friendship or my friendships with Chloe and Nicole. I didn't want a man with long dreads, gold teeth and a street boy from the North side.

My homegirl, Natalie and I were riding and I told her about the situation with Larry. I asked her for advice since she was best friends with Zoey, Chloe and I. She told me that she could understand why he would want me. I'm a good girl and I take care of my responsibilities, and he sees that. She could understand why I would like him because he did so much for Romelo and I. That will make you fall for anyone.

We both agreed that things happen and we were falling for each other, but it wasn't on purpose. I told her I was going to call Chloe and let her know and to see how she felt about the situation. Her feelings mattered, and I wanted to let her know before she heard anything in the streets. Apart of me wanted to keep it a secret because everybody already assumed we were talking since he was staying with me.

So, I called Chloe over to my house and we went outside and sat on the stairs. I told her about Larry and I. Then, I asked her how she felt about it, and if she didn't want me to talk to him, I wouldn't. She looked at me and said, "I already knew it because of how y'all act around each other. I feel like you're too good for him and he's not the kind of dude for you. You are a good mother and you take care of your son. But if you want to talk to him I'm okay with it."

I knew she really cared about me and I felt her response was genuine. I was relieved that we had sat down and talked. I never sat down with my cousin Nicole because I didn't think she would care because they didn't date that long. Maybe I should've still called her too because they still messed around. He told me that they weren't like that, but I kind of already knew what it was because I used to be around them. For some reason I was more concerned about Chloe though because we were together all of the time and hung with each other heavily. Nicole and I did too, but I guess it's really no excuse why I didn't sit her down too because it was more respectable to let them both know. Chloe seemed okay, so Larry and I made it official.

From that day forward we were together every day, all day. When you saw him, you saw me. Wherever he was, he'd call me to come. We were together 24/7 nonstop. He was in the house all of the time with me. He barely hung out on Basin Street doing his thing or hung out with his friends anymore. Whatever I wanted, he got it for me. He wanted to be up under me all of the time, and I loved it.

I was 21 and he was 23, and I fell in love with him fast. The feeling was mutual. He became my best friend and my lover. We had so much fun together. We even went out to clubs together. We didn't have any problems. It was all about us and nobody else mattered. Once everybody got wind that we were together, then there came the drama.

Everything changed between me and Chloe. She let others get in her ear about the situation, telling her that's nasty, I'm wrong, this and that. That changed her feelings about me and it wrecked our friendship. I was pissed because when she and I talked, she was okay with it. I felt I respected her enough to come to her first. But the fact that she let people get in her ear and change her feelings about me, I continued talking to him. Our friendship was over. Even with my other friend, Natalie, it was like she switched sides too once everybody started hearing about us. And that was the end of that friendship.

None of them were speaking to me anymore. At the time, I felt confused and hurt for losing my friends, but I was in love with Larry then. Even my friendship with my cousin was over too, even though we were blood-related. She was one of my closest cousins and I never meant to hurt her. I didn't even think it would affect her in the way that it did. She stopped talking to me, period. But Larry and I didn't break it off; we kept dating.

After a couple of months passed, he told me he wanted me to have his first child. I asked him, "Are you serious?" He said, "Yes, I honor you and respect how you take care of Romelo. You work hard and go to work every day to take care of y'all. Your dedication to Romelo, I love that."
I told him okay! He was so sweet and kind-hearted! I didn't care about his past or anything. I just focused on how he

treated me. From that point on, we had sex all of the time: day, night, and quickies-you name it, we did it all. I wanted to do whatever to make him happy.

It didn't take long. I got pregnant about a month later. We went to the doctor on November 14, 2003, my mother's birthday. Larry was filled with fever and tears of joy! Romelo was three years old at that time. Larry went around telling everybody I was pregnant. That was the most desirable day of his life. He wanted a baby so badly and his family knew that especially his oldest sister. When he told her, she said she wanted to see my paperwork because girls were always saying they were pregnant from him. Hahaha!! Too funny!

My mother wasn't happy at all, nor was my stepdad. They liked me and Larry being friends, but they didn't like us together at all. The fact that he was in the streets and sold drugs didn't fly with them at all. My oldest son's dad wasn't in his life, so they were very concerned about me being pregnant again.

But, It was all about Larry to me. He went to every doctor's appointment and he bought everything our baby needed. I didn't need to have a baby shower; he did everything. When I got farther along in my pregnancy, I noticed Larry started leaving the house and hanging out more. I figured because I was pregnant and couldn't move around like that, that he just wanted some hang out time with his friends. I didn't do anything but go to work and go home.

The hanging out became more and more heavy, and we started having arguments, that we never had before.

When I tried to go somewhere, he would get mad and tell me I couldn't do this or that. He started telling me what I couldn't wear and all kinds of stuff. I didn't know what was happening, but everything started changing. I don't know if it was because he was becoming a dad or if this was the real him.

When I called his phone, he'd answer and say he was busy getting money. We weren't spending that much time together anymore and I became very emotional and miserable. Nights passed and I was home alone. We had become distant staying in the same house. I thought this was supposed to be happy moments for both of us.

The day I found out what I was having, he made time to come, and of course, he was joyous when the doctor told us it was a boy. He went out and bought more stuff to add to all of the stuff he had already bought when he first found out I was pregnant. And he couldn't wait to let the world know it was a boy. He wanted the baby to have his name and all, which was no problem; this was his first son.

I was getting bigger and bigger and even started having complications. I went into labor early had to be hospitalized for a couple of days. I was in and out of the hospital with this baby. He wasn't playing and was trying to come out early. I ended up getting put on bed rest and went on maternity leave at six months. I didn't want to do it because I had bills to pay and Larry didn't work like that, only hustled. Larry told me to do what the doctor said and don't worry about it. He'd take of care of the bills. That was a blessing and so sweet of him. I appreciated him doing that for me.

My pregnancy started getting more complicated and the doctor had to stitch me up to keep the baby in there longer. It was so stressful and depressing. I was irritated by all of this and more irritated because Larry still didn't stay home with me. I needed him there at the house. I used to call his phone, going off about him not being there, and he would always say, "I'm getting money." Until I found out he was doing more than getting money.

I started hearing that he was messing with this and that girl. I didn't assume that at first. I just thought it was because I was pregnant and he just wanted to hang out.

I was home pregnant and he was out entertaining other females. So I got more aggravated, and my attitude changed quickly. It got to the point where I started going through his phone when he was asleep. I wanted to see what he was doing since he claimed he was always getting money. And I saw all kinds of text messages and pictures. This didn't do anything but hurt me more. I tried to stay focused because I was already high risk, aggravated with this pregnancy and dealing with Larry.

I used to walk the neighborhood, doing everything I could do to speed up the process and make the baby come naturally. Larry wouldn't be home and I would call him to come home because I was having pain, contractions, and everything else. He would say, "I'm on the way," but never showed up, and once again when I call him again he wouldn't answer or his phone would go straight to voicemail.

Going into the eighth month of pregnancy, the doctor finally decided to schedule me for a cesarean section. So on July

14, 2004, another bundle of joy was born, Larry Jr... Larry Sr. was there from the beginning to the end at delivery! He cried real tears. I'd never seen him smile, laugh, or cry the way he did when his son was born. And I'm not going to lie, I was overjoyed to share that moment with him. I always wanted to make him happy any way possible that I could. So that was a great moment for me just giving him a great moment to remember. That connection was priceless.

Our relationship was not good, but it didn't matter at that point. Larry had left the hospital and I started receiving calls saying he had already gone out and gotten a tattoo on his neck of his son's name. When it came time for us to go home, Larry picked us up. He wanted to show off his baby boy and I just wanted to get home. We finally got home and Larry helped get us all settled in along with my mother. He told me he'd be back. I just wanted to be home with both of my boys.

As night came there was no sign of Larry. I was calling his phone and texting him, but I got no response. I was on medication so I eventually fell asleep. When I woke up the next morning Larry wasn't there. He hadn't come home or called. Yes, I was pissed! This is the first night his son was home and I just had a C-section, and he didn't even come back to the house or call to see if we were OK. He already knew how I got in those situations, but he was expecting me to be sweet and nice.

Later on that day, he finally came over. I went off on him because that was not right at all. I found out he went out that night. That made me even madder. This was a repeat of our relationship over and over again. Having a baby from him didn't help or change anything. After a couple of months, I went back to work and he was watching our son. Some days I would go and some days I didn't. I was a lost child in this relationship and in my life.

It was this one guy that used to try and get with me all of the time. We actually used to talk when we were little and in middle school. His name was Tyler, and he was from the North side too. We had always been cool friends, he knew Larry too. I used to tell Larry all of the time that he was still trying to talk to me and was always calling my phone and texting, even while Larry and I were together. I used to ignore his calls and messages because of the fact that Larry and I were together.

Tyler even went out of his way to call other people to tell them to tell me he was trying to get in touch with me. He was really trying to get with me that bad. That was crazy! I guess he used to see Larry out when he was doing all of his dirt with the girls, and whatever else they used to do all night clubbing. I don't know if he figured Larry was doing me wrong and he didn't care about me or what. But one night Tyler called me during a time I was pissed, drained, and fed up with Larry. And to be real I don't even know if we were together or not. Our relationship was crazy, weird and full of childishness.

Anyway, I answered the phone this time. He asked if he could see me and we just hang for a little. At first, I told him no, but he kept asking and I said, "Yes." So he came over to pick me up. My cousin and godsister Erin watched Larry, Jr. for me because Romelo was with my sister, Lisa. Larry, Jr. was a year old around this time.

So, we rode around Tallahassee talking and laughing. Then he asked did I want to go to a hotel and chill. I already knew what time it was but I was so upset, irritated and pissed with Larry, so I said yeah. We went and chilled, and then we had sex. At the time, I didn't think about Larry until after it was over and Tyler took me back home that night. I treated that night and Tyler just like a one night stand. I pulled a dude move because I didn't talk, text or converse with him anymore. I went back to ignoring all his messages and I saw him plenty of times after that because we had lots of mutual friends.

I never told anyone about that night and I don't think he did. I don't even know if Larry ever heard or found out. I treated it like it never happened. Things didn't get better or worse for me and Larry; it stayed the same. Off and on, back and forth! That was our life and how we were living. He couldn't leave me alone and I couldn't leave him alone. It had been almost two years since we had our first child together.

CHAPTER 7

OVERWHELMED WITH CHOICES

It wasn't long before I was pregnant again with baby number three on the way. I was working hard, taking care of two boys, and trying to manage this so-called relationship with Larry. It wasn't easy because I was also keeping the household together. It was a lot going on; I was caught off guard with this pregnancy not being planned at all.

I knew that if we were going to bring another child into this world, then things needed to change between us. This started off an overwhelming situation. Everything I did from that point on was not all about me. I had to make choices, not only for myself, but for my boys as well. Things had gotten so out of hand in my household in different ways. Everything had become too much for me. Larry was staying out late and not coming or calling to see if the kids and I were okay. The life we created wasn't well put together, but I tried my very best to live a good life.

Larry was keeping our son at home at the time because daycare was too much for me to pay and he wasn't working. He would stay out all night knowing he had to keep our son, and at the last minute, I had to find a babysitter. I would call his phone, but there was no answer. A few days later he would show up to my apartment. For him, that was okay, but not so much for me.

I couldn't keep dealing with that kind of stuff, especially being pregnant at the time. We ended up talking with his mother to see if she could start watching Larry Jr. for us. That was much better because she was a more reliable babysitter than him.

Soon after, Larry had finally got a call about a job working at this place called the Rose Printing Company . I was very excited because he needed to work because I needed the help. I was hoping this would calm him down and stop all the hanging out he'd been doing. "It's going to get better," is what I used to tell myself all the time. A couple of months went by and we were doing well. He was home the majority of the time. With his new job he had to work from 2-10 p.m. I would go to work at 4:50 a.m. and then go home to take him to work on my lunch break. We had a routine.

After I got off, I would go to pick Larry Jr. up from the babysitter because Romelo rode the bus with me. I was still a bus assistant on the school bus, so that definitely worked for me already having one of my children with me. Once the boys and I got home, I would cook dinner, clean, get the boys bathed and ready for bed. I would shower around 9:30 at night, then wake the boys up so that we could go get Larry from work. This was our daily routine.

One Tuesday, I took off from work because I wasn't feeling very well. By then, I was about seven months along in my pregnancy. Larry and I chilled, laughed and talked until it was time for him to go to work.

We got up about 1:15 p.m. and I took him to work, and when he got ready to get out of the car, he told me I didn't have to pick him up later that night. He had a ride home, and I said, "OK."

I went back home, got the boys situated, and cooked dinner. After I put the boys to bed I went to sleep. I woke up in the middle of the night to go use the restroom—"pregnancy life." I stayed up a little while to see what time he was going to come home, but he never showed up. So, I went back to sleep. I got up for work the next morning and he still wasn't there, and I had no clue where he was. And to be honest, I didn't care, but it didn't take a rocket scientist to figure out what Larry was out doing. He was cheating, and I was sure of it.

One day turned into two and I still hadn't heard from nor seen him. Two weeks went by and I still hadn't heard from him. I even called a girl who he called his sister asking if she had seen or heard from him. Of course, she said no. I told her if she did see him to tell him to call me. I knew that she knew where he was because they were very close and he always talked to her or was at her house.

After sitting and thinking over all of the mess that he was doing, I became extremely pissed and miserable. I packed all of his clothes and called my stepdad Joe, to tell him everything that was going on. I asked him to come help me get all of Larry's clothes out of my house and drop it off to his mother's house.

Then, I put all of his things in trash bags. I was so irritated that I got a gallon of bleach and poured it all over his clothes and shoes. That was very childish of me but I didn't care about that at the time. Once my stepdad arrived, he agreed with me about getting his stuff out of my house because my parents had enough of his nonsense as well. Pregnant and all, I was over and done with this foolishness that came with him. We took his stuff to his mother's house and left it on the porch in front of her door.

I didn't knock or anything. I thought they would see it whenever they come outside. I didn't feel sad or bad about what I had done to his stuff. I was to the point where I didn't care if I was going through the pregnancy alone. Outsiders always used to tell me, "He ain't nothing." But I wouldn't listen. I prayed for him to be the person he was when we first met. He was a sweet person but his actions made him so awful. A couple of days later, I received a call from his mother who was mad and going off about his clothes. She was so upset that I had bleached his clothes and left them on her porch.

All I could do was laugh at her and him. I thought to myself, *Oh well this will teach him a lesson and let him know I'm through with him*. I guess his mother was able to reach him to tell him about his clothes . Most definitely he was pissed and we didn't talk for a while after that period. He didn't call me and I didn't call him.

His oldest sister and I would talk all of the time because she felt my pain. She used to tell me to not worry about it; just focus on myself because I was pregnant. We were very close and I appreciated her for always being there for me when I needed a shoulder. At that time, she never got in between our mess but she would be there whenever I called her. I was tired of going through stuff with Larry.

Things were worse during that pregnancy than my first by him. I knew we were both in our 20's, so I thought maybe he was still trying to figure things out and didn't want to give up hanging out all day and night just yet. For a bit, I dealt with it as long as I could, but I couldn't do it. I was close to having our son and I needed him there. My due date was approaching and it was time for me to go on maternity leave. I still hadn't heard from Larry, not even to check up on his other son. Stress was really taking over me.

Everyone knows I'm not good at dealing with things because I get so stressed out. My feet were swollen and there was pain all over my body. I could barely walk or do anything around the house. My mother, my sister and his oldest sister would come over and help me out when they could. Our son Larry Jr. needed diapers and I couldn't go get them, so his sister told me, "Call his daddy." I told her I wasn't calling him because I didn't want to talk to him or see him. I asked her to call him for me and she did.

I guess he was waiting on a call because as soon as she called him, he came and brought the diapers. When he knocked on the door, I didn't let him in. I stood at the door and took the diapers. Then he asked to see his son Larry Jr.. So, I got his son and handed him over, then closed the door. I told him to knock when he was ready to hand him back to me. I didn't even want him in my house.
Another childish moment, but I didn't care. I know I was wrong for how I was acting. I was stressed out and my body

wasn't too happy about everything going on. I started having more and more pain and was cramping like crazy. The pain was unmanageable for me. I went to the emergency room and they admitted me into the hospital where they kept me for one night to monitor me and the baby.

The next day, my doctor told me that I was 37 weeks along in my pregnancy and the baby was seven pounds, so she was going to schedule me for an C-section. She scheduled me for two weeks away, which was December 6, 2006. I didn't want to be nasty even though Larry and I weren't talking, so I called him and let know when the C-section was scheduled.

We still didn't talk anymore after that. It had become normal for me, and even though I thought it should've been a relief, it had made me more stressed. He didn't call to check up on me to see how I was doing or anything. I put it in my mind that I was done with him and I wasn't going to deal with him anymore. It didn't matter if he called or not; I just needed to focus on what's going on at that point with me and my baby. I prepared myself for the C-section because those two weeks went by so fast, but it was good to have my mother by my side.

I called Larry the next day. To remind him of the scheduled C-section and he said "OK."

I started to call him when I got up the morning of the C-section, but I said no, I already called him yesterday to remind him. I got to the hospital about 4:45 a.m. They checked me in and began the process. There still was no call or sign of Larry anywhere. All I could think about was that I knew he was on the North side somewhere probably with some chick instead of being at the hospital with me. I tried not to think about it because my contractions were coming so fast and strong.

When it was time for them to take me into the surgery room, he still hadn't called or come up, so my mother went in the surgery room with me. My baby boy was born at 5:55 a.m., and I was beaming with anger. He had missed the delivery of our son but it didn't have any impact on what had happened. My baby boy was there and healthy as ever. He was one of the most precious babies ever. He was juicy, chocolate, and had silky black hair. That was just what I needed at the moment. He made me feel so much better.

It was sad his dad didn't see him come into this world. My mother kept telling me to get my tubes tied. Before I could say anything, she told the doctor to tie my tubes. I knew things weren't good between Larry and I, so I told them right then to go ahead and tie my tubes. I knew then I didn't want more kids; I was done and finished. Honestly, I didn't think on it or have time to. The stress of having three boys was enough for me. So I just agreed with it and got it done.

It kinda felt like that was the right thing to do. Larry and I weren't talking or together, so I went ahead and made that decision. Apparently word had gotten out to Larry that our son was here. He showed up to the hospital later that day all happy and excited. I wasn't happy to see him, and I'm sure he felt that. He had the nerve to ask me why I didn't call him and tell him our baby was here. I looked at him like he was crazy. Plus, my mother was there so I didn't want to say anything too outrageous. He sat there with his son for a while, holding him and kissing on him.

I was drugged up the whole time he was there because I was in pain. My sister, Lisa, had my other two boys and she brought them up to see me and their new brother. One of my staples had come out and they had to staple my cut on my stomach again. I was so gloomy and displeased. I was in the hospital for two or three days, Larry came up there once.

I was surprised about that because he was there more when I had our first son. But you never know when it comes to Larry; he was living and doing his own thing in his own world by himself... or at least without us. When I got discharged I didn't call him to let him know. My mother came and took us home, and his sister met us at the house. Once we got all settled in, her brother called. He asked her where she was and she replied, "At Tenica's house."

He said, "What...they're home from the hospital?" And she told him, "Yes, they came home today."

He was pissed because I didn't call and tell him. I was done calling and texting him. About 10 minutes after that, we heard a knock on the door. My mother asked, "Who can that be? You just got home."

Well, it was Larry! He came in all jolly and happy as usual like nothing happened, just started playing with his son and holding him. Then my sister brought my boys home. In the meantime, I put my anger to the side and let everyone enjoy the moment. It had been a long few days, so I just wanted some rest. Larry and I started communicating a lot more after Ross was born. I needed more help with my other boys as well. So it wasn't long before Larry had moved back in with us. We were back together and things were going pretty great. Whenever he was out I would call and say the boys needed this or that and he would go get it and bring it straight to the house.

I was loving that, so there was no need for me to fuss or argue about anything. He was helping out a lot more and he told me that he wanted to be there for me throughout my pregnancy, but I wouldn't let him. You could see he was trying to make things easier for me by taking Romelo to school and picking him up. I was in a happy place and he was too. When he would leave he would call and check up on the kids and me to make sure we were okay or if we needed anything.

All of that made me happy. Eventually, we moved into a new townhouse that was bigger. I went back to work and he wasn't working again. He was waiting on Trojan Labor to find him something else. He didn't like the Rose Printing job because of the night shift, and that was okay with me because I was used to taking care of everything and him helping when he can or when he wanted to.

He would drop me off to work and keep the car until it was time for me to get off. The kids would go with me because they were able to ride the school bus with me. After he got me from work, he would drop us at home then go hang out on Basin Street. This was an everyday thing since he wasn't working. I didn't say anything at first, but then I noticed him staying out later and not answering my calls again.

Sometimes he would call back and sometimes he would just ignore my calls. That would start arguments and I began to have an attitude again with him. When he did come home late, his phone would ring all night. One night, he came home with two phones and he tried to hide it, but I found it. He said he bought the phone, but I later found out a chick bought it for him.

Once, I found some condoms in the car. He said that his homeboy had left them in there, which I knew was a lie. Things were all messed up again. It was because of this popular social media site that everyone had, including us. One day, he left his MySpace page open. So looked at it. I saw where some chick was asking him, "What he was going to do about his situation?" I typed back pretending to be him and asked her, "What situation?"

She was kind of hesitant about saying what it was, like she knew it wasn't him. I had to get her to talk. So, I had to make her feel like it was him. I typed back, "I'm lost for real?"

She replied, "About the baby."

My heart dropped, and all I could do was stare at the computer screen, thinking I know she didn't just say what I thought she said. I felt like I couldn't breathe anymore. So I just typed back, "I didn't know about the baby, but thank you anyway. This is Larry's baby mama."

Then she logged off. I called his phone so fast I was shaking. When he answered I could barely talk to him I told him to come to the house now. Now, so he came.

I asked him about what the girl had said, and all he could say was why was I looking on his MySpace? Then he went on to say, "What girl?" and that he didn't know what I was talking about. I told him to look on his MySpace, and when he did, he still said he didn't know what I was upset about. We argued and then he left in my car.

I was so upset, and all I could do was cry, thinking about him having another baby from somebody and knowing I just had a baby from him. I called his sister immediately and told her. She was trying to calm me down and tell me she hadn't heard anything about that. I had to find out if this was true or not because Larry wasn't going to tell the truth. I called our close friend Levi and I told him what had happened. He was shocked at first, but then he told me it's true. Wow!

He told me that Larry had told him two weeks prior that he messed up and that he thought a chick named Kara was pregnant. And he didn't know how to tell me or what to do because he knew it was going to hurt me. Then I asked, "Who was Kara?"

He told me she was a young girl, about 19, who hung out on Basin Street. That made me more pissed because Larry was messing with an 19 year old and he was 27. I called his phone and I told him to bring me my car and for him to get his things out of my house. Some people thought that I was wrong and overreacting.

I wouldn't let him see his kids or anything. I wasn't answering any calls from him. I made other arrangements for my kids when I needed someone to watch them. All I kept hearing was his homegirls and some family members saying I was being childish and I wouldn't let him see his kids. It's funny how everyone wants you to always remain the bigger person in every situation. People always have their thoughts and opinions on your situation until it becomes their situation.

My attitude level was on high and my mouth was nonstop every time someone brought his name up to me. I don't know how someone could think I was just going to be quiet and just let him run all over me and do me wrong when I'm the mother of his children. That's how guys think though. He thought I was being so wrong and nasty to him. Dudes just don't care, especially the ones from the streets. I had a bad taste about some of the dudes from the North side because of how they all were with females.

For some odd reason we couldn't leave them alone. Like I had mentioned before, we were both young with kids trying to live adult lives. Yes, you can be in your 20s and still not fully be mature for adult relationships. My brain would be racing so many nights trying to figure out how to change myself and I.

I knew I loved him and didn't want anyone else and definitely didn't want him to have anyone else! It's sad because Larry would literally take my car all day and night. I wouldn't see him until I woke up, or the following day. I'm sure plenty of girls had been in my car because that's all he was doing at night, and sheesh, during the day too. The girls he messed with were never mature women, unfortunately. I just put up with so much stuff because I didn't want him to go anywhere else other than with me.

I was paying most of the bills in the house and holding us down. All he could do was be out cheating on me all of the time. I've always been independent, although my mother and stepfather would help me out whenever I needed it. And my sister Lisa would help whenever she wasn't mad or in her feelings about me being with Larry. She disliked him so much because of all the things he did to me and the fact she use to see him out doing it. Sometimes she knew the females he was doing it with. I never felt like that should determine what she did for me and her nephews. People think so differently.

You're supposed to love your siblings no matter what and help them out if they need you. But it didn't matter to me. I wasn't going to leave Larry. I did sometimes, but we all know how that goes: they're gone for a minute and you're done... then they're right back with you, staying in your house, having sex with you and all. This is something that the majority of females do, especially when it comes to their kids' dad.

I didn't let too many people know about the baby, but word travels fast in Tallahassee. Larry and I weren't on good terms at all. I wasn't even in the townhouse long and I moved into an apartment on the South side of town. I called him to help move my stuff because I didn't have anyone else to move it. He tried to talk to me about the baby situation, but I felt everything that came out his mouth was a lie. I didn't want to hear any lies. The streets knew the truth more than I did. Once again, I was over the cheating and stuff. I just wanted to be happy.

Tenica Cofield

Once I was settled in my new apartment, I asked him to move back in with me. I missed him and I wanted him there with me. This was something that I did all of the time, take him back over and over again.

I complained all of the time to myself and some friends, but I always took him back or wanted him back in the house. I used the kids as an excuse to get him back in the house if I needed, too. We were having our ups and downs. He felt like I fussed too much, and sometimes I did. I wanted him to stop all of the stuff he was doing in the streets.

By this time , I was 27 and he was 29, and we had grown together. No one really understood us, but we did. We shared something so sweet and weird, but some would call it STUPID! I kept putting in my mind how much I loved him. I know other females go through stuff with their kids' dads all of the time and nobody understands them, but them. I tried to make everything okay after every situation.

Sometimes he made me feel like I was on top of the world and sometimes he just knocked me down. Thoughts of being without him drove me crazy and I wanted him around all of the time. I tried to not think about the girl being pregnant anymore. Every now and then I would think about it or talk about it, but I did my best to convince myself it wasn't true.

The arguments didn't stop for long; we were back at it again and again. Female after female, and all of this disrespect, rudeness and hanging out. The longer we stayed together, the more we argued. We got along for maybe 30 seconds, if that. We broke up again, and this time I started talking to someone else. It was this dude from down South who was real good friends with one of my cousins. He always tried to talk to me whenever he saw me, but I wouldn't talk to him. I would always just laugh and smile at him. He came over to my house one time with my cousin when I did her hair. Doing hair was my little side hustle. Anyway, I gave in to him and let him have my phone number. His name was Jit and he was a real cool dude.

I could talk to him about any and everything. He gave me so much good advice on a lot of things. He was sweet and made me smile all of the time. We started talking, hanging and chilling heavy. Whatever I needed or wanted, he made sure I had it. We talked about everything and he looked out for my kids as well. He seemed so different. He always made sure I was OK and good. He was one of the homies to me because we vibed so good.

He had spoiled me. That's what I needed: no drama, just straight chill. We started having sex and things started to become heavy with us. Whenever I took the kids out for some fun, he would always pay for it. One day, I took them skating and he came out to pay for it. This was the day my kids' dad wanted to get them but I had already planned to take them skating with his oldest sister. This was the first time Jit ever saw my kids, but I didn't mind because I wasn't going back to their dad because we were done.

My kids went with their dad that next day to spend time with him, since I took them skating the day before. As soon as I dropped them off to him and got back home, I received a phone called from Larry asking me, "Who was my friend?"

I asked him what he meant. He said our baby boy asked him if he knew mommy's friend. So I lied to him and told him it was nobody. And we left it at that. He didn't like that at all. He acted like he was going crazy because somebody was around his kids and I was talking to somebody, which he thought I would never do. He called me saying how he wanted his family back and crying about this and that. He even went all out and called my mother about me talking to another dude. Larry made it such a big deal. So just like that, I broke a good thing off with Jit and took Larry back. He moved back in with us.

Jit wasn't happy and was confused about why I was taking him back after all the stuff he had done to me. I felt so stupid but I was crazy in love with Larry. No matter what he did and how many times he did it, I would take him back.

Jit and I remained friends because he liked and cared for me so much. I felt like I had done him so wrong, but he didn't hold that against me. He was still there for me and my kids no matter what. Larry had asked me some questions about Jit, but I wouldn't really tell him much besides his name and that he wasn't from Tallahassee. He wasn't, so I didn't lie about that. With all the drama that we had, I always just wanted us to be happy. I felt overwhelmed with the stress of his other chicks and me trying to figure out what to do about this and that. I was tired of being stressed out all of the time but I cared so much for Larry and my boys so I didn't change things. I wanted us to be a happy family.

CHAPTER 8
DOES MARRIAGE REALLY CHANGES THINGS?

Larry couldn't let go of the Jit situation. I thought he did because he didn't mention it anymore. On the 4th of July, 2009, we went over to my dad's house for a cookout. We chilled, laugh, ate good and did fireworks. It was such a great day spending time with family. Larry and my dad were drinking and talking. Whenever we went over to my dad's house, he would always send his girlfriend to the store to get some beer for Larry to drink. After a long day we went home, and everything was fine.

Once we got in the house, I put the kids to bed. When I walked back in my room, Larry asked me, "Now who is this Jit nigga?"

I looked at him and said, "Boy, whatever, we are not about to talk about that. Plus, you're drunk and I have work in the morning. I'm going to bed."

Then he came and stood in front of me and said, "I'm going to ask you one more time because I found out who he was. My other sister knows the dude and she already told me, so you better tell me the truth!"
I just looked at him and said, "He was just my friend."

Things got out of hand and we started arguing loudly. He reached in the drawer and got his gun. He asked me, "Did you have sex with that nigga?"

I said, "No."

I was not about to tell him because he was drunk, had a temper, and I knew if I said yes he would kill me. By then I was scared and crying. My kids were right down the hallway in their rooms. Our room door was open. He said, "You're lying. I'm going to ask you one more time."

I asked him to please stop, the kids were there, and I kept saying that. He told me he didn't care. He said, "I'm going to ask you one more time, and this is your last chance to answer."

He cocked the gun back to put a bullet in and put it to my head. I thought my life was over. Everything was black, and I think I went deaf for a minute because I couldn't hear anything. I started crying more saying, "Please don't kill me, please don't shoot me."

Then he said, "Oh now you want to cry."

After a couple of minutes he pulled the gun from my face, and soon as he did that, I grabbed my car keys and ran out the house. I didn't want to leave my kids but I knew he wasn't going to hurt them. I didn't know what to do or where to go, so I drove around crying and shaking. I didn't call anybody. I couldn't believe what had just happened. All I could think about was the sound of the gun being cocked back and put to my head.

My phone started ringing and it was a number I didn't know. I didn't answer but they kept calling. So I answered the phone and the lady said it was the Tallahassee Police Department. They told me they got a call from my oldest son. They asked me where I was and said that I needed to get back to the house now. When I arrived at my apartment complex, police were everywhere. As I walked up the stairs, the police started asking me questions and asking what happen. I told them we got into an argument and I left so that I could cool down. The lady told me that my oldest son said that Larry had a gun to my head, was about to shoot me, and he heard me screaming "don't shoot me don't shoot me." The officer asked, "Is this true?"

My head dropped with tears rolling down my face. I was scared and afraid of what was about to happen. Romelo was right there looking at me and he was scared and crying. I didn't want Larry to go to jail and I didn't want to call my son a liar. I answered, "No, that's not true! We were fussing but there wasn't a gun involved."

They took Larry outside and told him, "We're going to ask you again. Did you have a gun and were you about to shoot her?" He said, "No, sir I don't have a gun." My son looked at me and said, "Yes! It was a gun."

I told my son there was no gun and that's not what you heard. That was so painful and I was so disgusted with myself for lying. My child was trying to save my life and I put Larry before him and myself.

They searched the apartment for the gun but couldn't find it. He had hidden it in the dryer under the white clothes. That was a terrifying night and I was so hurt for myself, my kids and Larry. I blamed myself for everything that had happened. I should've just told him the truth. So many things were going through my head. They made Larry leave for the night. They said Larry couldn't be in the house until the investigation was over which was for 45 days.

I had to make up a lie to tell my mother and my neighbors. Until this day, nobody knows whatever happened to us. Only the made-up story because my landlord stayed downstairs from me in my building. I almost lost my life and children for that dude because I was so caught up in loving him and wanting to be with him so badly. Someone had to come in and out of my home for 45 days and then they finally closed the case. Larry was mad because he couldn't stay in the house.

I was so embarrassed, ashamed, lost, hurt, and felt so stupid. But like always, I apologized to him about everything—for messing with Jit, and I even apologized for him messing with all of the chicks he was messing with. I wanted all this to be behind us and we move forward. I had so many nightmares of him putting the gun to my face.

I don't know if these nightmares will ever go away. When you are going through so much in a relationship, you try to figure out all kinds of solutions. How to fix the problem or what to do to make it better. Females go crazy when things are so messed up in their relationship. Trying to figure out things like *is it really over? Is he really done this time? Do I really want to be with him? Am I stupid for putting up with all the cheating and drama?* No matter how bad he had done me and all the stuff he had done, I still didn't want him to go.

We had been together for nearly 10 years, and I was not just about to give that up. This rumor was still going around that he had a baby from the young chick, but of course I stayed with him and stayed by his side the whole time during the pregnancy. After everything that had happened to us those past months, I found out that he was still messing around with the young girl while she was pregnant.

My love for Larry was so real. I just had to figure out a way to get him away from these females and away from all that fighting we had done. I felt as if he was the air I breathed. He was my oxygen. I couldn't sleep without him and sometimes I felt as if I couldn't think either. When things went wrong, he was never the one to try to fix things.

It was an it-is-what-it-is situation with him. So many people were in our business, and a lot of our business were put out by both of us. Our relationship was a hot mess! There was no respect there. I don't know if we were just holding on to each other because we had kids together. That was one of the ways females think we can stop a man from leaving. Or by getting pregnant or because we have his kids. I knew I had to think outside the box. I waited up one night on Larry to get home so we could talk. He put everything out there about the chick being pregnant and all the cheating he'd been doing.

He finally told me that it's a possibility that the baby could be his baby. It was kind of a relief, but it still hurt to hear that.

I didn't know what to say when he said those words, but I already knew that anyway. I surprised him with my reply: "If the baby is yours then I'm going to accept that baby. Even though you were cheating and got the baby, I'm going to love it like it's mine. That's my kids' sibling so I'm going to be okay with the baby."

I don't know if I really meant that or not, but I didn't want to lose him. Deep down inside that's not how I really felt, but I had to say something that he wanted to hear because I wanted to make it okay for him. I knew that was something crazy and stupid to say, but I was in love with him. My heart was hurting inside and he had no idea. Larry asked me, "Are you sure?"

And I said, "Yes."

I think he knew I was lying or didn't really mean that because he was just staring me in my eyes. But he just said, "OK," then went on to say that he didn't talk to her anymore and that he was going to just wait until they got a blood test before he did anything. Everything he was saying went in one ear and out the other. I just wanted to be with him. I don't know if this is what you call "blinded by love" or just plain stupid, but that was me, always trying to make things okay and letting a lot of things happen and slide.

I might fuss about some things, but I never held any grudges against him. I would get mad at him one moment and then five minutes later I would be talking to him like nothing ever happened. But he was different. He held on to grudges and the things I fussed about.

One day, it came to me that maybe we should talk about getting married. We had a sit-down talk about marriage before when he was locked up in jail, but we never got married. I knew I didn't want to bring that up that night because we had just had the discussion about the baby possibility being his and the cheating he'd been doing. We talked some things out and were on the same page.

I felt I had to think about it for a couple of days to see if I was really ready for marriage or if I knew anything about getting married. My mother was married and I watched her, but no one actually taught me about being a wife, and no one taught him about being a husband. It seemed as if all the young people were just getting married anyway. One of his homeboys had just gotten married the year before. Plus, he was supposed to be getting the DNA test done on the baby. I didn't want to pressure him but I didn't want to hold it off too much longer. The next day, Larry and I were riding in the car and I asked him what he thought about us getting married. He replied, "Yes, I want to get married."

He looked at me and said, "Do you want to get married?" Of course I said, "Yes!" I was willing to do whatever I could so he wouldn't leave me and so we could stay together. We decided to get married. Larry didn't have a job or anything, but I didn't care. He did his hustling thing on the side at the time because he had lost his job that he had through Trojan Labor. It was cool though. I gave him the money to buy the ring.

I know it sounds crazy, but there are a lot of women out there who pay for their own ring. You would definitely be surprised at how many there actually are. It may sound dumb to a lot of people, but this happens all of the time.

Larry dropped me off at work and then went to look for a ring for me. He would send me pics while I was at work so I would see the ones he picked out.

When I got off, he took me by some of the places so I could see and try them on. There was one that really stood out, and it wasn't that expensive at all. It was at the pawnshop on the South side of town. When I tried it on, it fit perfectly, but we didn't get it that day. Larry actually went back and got the ring without letting me know.

He asked me to marry him on Valentine's Day, February 14, 2010. I was so happy! You couldn't tell me anything. Some of my friends and I weren't on good terms, so I really didn't have anybody to call and tell. They didn't like me with him for all the stuff he had done and was still doing to me, which I felt was very wrong in a way. No matter whom your friend dates or what they go through with their significant other, you're still supposed to always be there for them.

That's what real friends do. Real friends don't get mad at you and stop talking to you because of the decisions you've made. Nobody's perfect and we all love differently. Dudes have done us all wrong in different situations. No situation is better than the other. I was never judgmental when it came to my friends' dudes or situations with them.

It's okay to give your opinion and advice, but getting mad with that person and talking about the decisions they've made isn't cool. So I unfriended them and they unfriended me. They looked at it and told everyone that I picked Larry over them, which wasn't true. At the end of the day they were my friends, not Larry's friends. Some of them had been cheated on and mistreated badly, but I never judged them for staying or going back. I may have said things or given my opinion or advice, but I didn't get mad over whatever decision they made.

I always felt that my friends were so judgmental when it came to my relationship, so what was a happy moment for me, I decided to not share with them. They found out however they found out. Many days had gone by before I told anyone. Some people found out just by seeing the ring on my finger. Word travels fast around Tallahassee, so it wasn't long before everybody knew we were engaged. One of his sisters wasn't happy at all, but we weren't expecting everyone to be happy for us. She didn't like me anyway, and it didn't bother me at all.

When my mother found out she was happy for us. She was a praying woman, and she always kept us in her prayers and tried to lead and guide us in the right direction. She knew some of the things Larry had done and some of the things that he wasn't doing within the household. She also knew that my behavior wasn't always good either.

That didn't stop her love or prayers for him or us. She wanted us to have a wedding immediately and wanted to start planning the wedding. But Larry and I didn't want a wedding. We had already talked about going to the courthouse. After getting engaged in February, we went and applied for our marriage license and certificates, but when we got a copy of Larry's birth certificate, we found out that his last name was different from the one he was going by. That was definitely a bummer because Larry had no clue his last name was the same as his fathers. For 30 years he had been going by his mother's last name. Not to mention our two children had this same last name that he was going by.

That was beyond crazy!! His mother had no clue either. So he had to apply for a new social security card and we had to go in front of a judge to get our children's names changed. "That was definitely some ghetto mess," I told him.

We both laughed but were very blown away. That pushed the date back for us to get married at the courthouse. Once everything was fixed, we made our date for March 19, 2010. We were too excited! My mother wasn't too delighted with the whole courthouse decision.

We didn't care; it was all about us and what we wanted. It wasn't the perfect place to get married, but we couldn't afford a wedding. And I was in such a hurry. I don't know why I was rushing to be married. Maybe I thought Larry would change his mind. Nobody really knew we went up to the courthouse and applied for the marriage certificate and license or even knew the date we had picked. Without any friends or parents we were getting married. We needed some witnesses, so we had both of our oldest sisters and my hairstylists wife. Our kids weren't even there for the wedding.

Courthouse weddings were cheaper, quicker and easier. We got married that Friday at 10 am. The wedding didn't take long at all. It actually was pretty quick! I put on my prom dress from high school, and he put on his black dress pants, blue dress shirt and a tie. After our ceremony, we left off for our honeymoon in Panama City Beach, Florida. My mother got the kids from school and kept them for that weekend.

Larry stopped by the liquor store and got us a bottle of Gin and he rounded us up a nice blunt or two, and we were ready for sure. It was just us two, and we were so happy and excited. At every stop we made, we let people know that we had just gotten married. I was in heaven. I had just gotten married to my best friend, babies' dad and lover. I just knew and felt that all of our problems were done and over with.

He was through with all the girls, cheating, staying out all night, not coming home, the disrespect and name-calling. The feeling felt so different that weekend, and it was a moment I wanted for life. We stayed out on the beach, enjoying each other's company and laughed, just living in the moment, celebrating our new beginnings with each other. It was one of the best weekends we had ever had with one another. There was no fighting or arguing. Just love, laughs and fun.

Eventually, our fun weekend came to an end. We had to head back home to our kids. The first week of our marriage felt great. Our neighbors surprised us when we arrived back home. One of our favorite couples were our neighbors and the landlords of the apartment complex where we stayed. The wife had surprised me with a bridal shower, and her husband had surprised Larry with a trip to Gainesville, Florida.
We weren't expecting that because a lot of people weren't happy about us getting married. We didn't get too many

"Congratulations" because nobody wanted us to be married. So many people thought he wasn't good enough for me, and a lot of people thought I wasn't good enough for him, especially a lot of the females who he had messed around with or who had crushes on him. Ever since we started dating, a lot of the females in the city didn't like me with him at all. They were very jealous! Trust and believe people would say things like, "She think she got something" or "He's nothing but a hoe." But they still wanted him. None of that mattered to me because we were married and I was his "wifey."

I changed a lot of things for my marriage. I wasn't hanging with anyone like that or really going out anymore. I went to work, took care of the boys, cooked , cleaned and made sure I gave him as much sex as possible. I even stopped fussing so much about what he did or didn't do. One of our problems was that I always had something to say when he stayed out or when he hung on Basin Street. I just put all of that on the back burner and focused on our new married life. Everything seemed to be going well the first couple of weeks. Larry even had gotten a job working through Trojan Labor again for the City of Tallahassee. You definitely couldn't tell me anything at that point for sure.

We were like this little happy family. It wasn't before long that he started hanging out in the projects with his friends. I wasn't too happy about that because that's where mostly everything goes down at. I didn't like him hanging out over there at all. Yes, he had family over there, but I didn't care. All I could think about was all the cheating he done over there, staying out it, and not coming home. He finally got the letter to go take the DNA test for the little girl. Luckily, it came back to not be his baby, so I didn't have to put up with that. That actually was good news to me. The Devil doesn't want to see you happy, and some people just can't do right at all. They will have something good and they would rather throw it all away.

Larry was a big drinker and smoker. He drank beer every day and liquor on the weekends. After I got off work, I would go pick up the kids from daycare and rush to pick him up from work. If I was late even a minute or two, he would go off and be pissed off at me.

On the days I would be late or piss him off, he would stay out all day and night. On weekdays, he would drop me and the kids off at the house and go straight to Basin Street, and hang out there for the rest of the day and night. I would cook dinner and get the kids off to bed and he would not be there. I used to call his phone asking him when he was coming home. Sometimes he wouldn't even answer my calls at all. I would call back to back, and he still would not answer the phone. I used to be pissed because we were married. I was his wife and he was supposed to always answer, but that didn't mean anything to him. He came in when he wanted to and did what he pleased. I went to get my hair done and my hairstylist told me that a friend of Larry and mine told him some things. So I asked him "What?"

He told me that she said that our baby boy wasn't my husband's son. That she was pregnant by my husband before and lost the baby. That she liked and dated my husband first, and that she was mad at me for dating him. My mouth dropped because first of all I had no idea that they were dating because she used to date his cousin.

I told my hairstylist, "Not only that. She and his cousin are supposed to have had a child together. I knew she use to have a crush on him because we have had that conversation, but I didn't know they ever messed around."

The part about my son not being his baby was a lie, but she told my hairstylist that she heard it from the dude's mouth who was supposedly the daddy, saying that my baby boy wasn't Larry's baby. I was so furious that my legs and hands were shaking. I wanted him to hurry up with my hair.

We had just gotten married! We we're husband and wife is all I could think about. As soon as I left the hair salon, I called Larry's phone. He was at work. I told him everything that was just told to me. Then I asked him was any of this true, especially about her being pregnant and losing the baby. His reply was, "Bitch, if that's what she said, then that's what it is!"

All I could say was, "Are you serious right now?

Larry, this is me, your wife and your kids' mother. How could you say and talk to me like that?" He kept saying if that's what she told my hairstylist then that's what it was, and yes, he'd heard that our younger baby wasn't his baby. He started calling me "pussy hoe", "nasty hoe", and said he didn't want to be with me and that he was moving out of the house. He said he didn't give a fuck about a marriage. All I could do was cry and go back off on him telling him how nasty he was for doing that to me. Also that he was a trifling ass nigga who needed to get his shit out of my house.

It was sad but that's how we carried on and talked to each other. That was horrible for a husband and wife. We went back and forth on the phone, until he eventually hung up on me. I kept calling and calling liar and evil. By then I started calling him all kinds of names—fuck nigga, deadbeat, liar, and evil. The things we were saying to each other were crazy and so disrespectful.

I went back to work. I couldn't even think straight. My mind was all over the place, and my heart was hurting so bad. I just kept saying to myself, "How could he do this to me? How could he say these things to me? I'm his wife; we're supposed to be best friends."

We weren't married a whole three months and he was already moving out of the house. It was so sad because I felt so stupid because I just knew us getting married would change our lives and relationship.

He was going to love only me, cherish only me, change how he treated me and be with me and the kids only. I thought that everything was going to be so sweet and lovely. He moved out and one of his sisters got involved. She didn't like me anyway, so she was nasty about this because she started spreading the rumors around about him not being the daddy of our baby boy. She was telling people I wasn't shit, I was sneaky, and that I thought I was all of that.

So many people told me that she said her brother only married me because of the kids. I thought our relationship was already a mess before marriage, but I was fooled! This situation became a bigger mess, and our family and friends were involved now. Outsiders were making it worse, and so did he because he really started messing with females all over the city when he moved out.

This was beyond crazy! This wasn't our marriage or problem anymore; it was everyones. I used to sit up, call and text his phone every day, and he wouldn't answer or respond. My mother and some friends told me to just leave it alone. As days, weeks, and months went by, we were barely talking or doing any communicating. We weren't married a year and had already been apart for four months.

He was staying with his sister and no telling who else. Christmas was coming up and we had to get a couple of things for the kids. So, we starting seeing each other more and we spent Christmas shopping together. He slowly moved back in. We talked and I apologized to him for what happened and the things I said to him. I even apologized to him for his behavior. Yes, this was something that I always did, apologize when I was wrong and not wrong just so we could move forward with our problems and be on good terms.

Larry and I brought the New Year in together, putting our differences to the side and trying to get along. People thought I was insane for letting him move back in after he just up and moved out. My hairstylist thought he was such a coward how he handled the whole situation. He even called him to talk to him, but Larry hung the phone up. I was over the drama! Larry knew that Ross was his son, so there was no need to continue on about it.

When he came back that Christmas, he told me just that. He never thought that Ross wasn't his child and he didn't care what his sister said... period. Like I said before, we just let it all go and went into the new year together.

CHAPTER 9
NEW LIFE...OLD WAYS

Bringing in the new year together and putting our differences to the side...trying to get along. I didn't want to think about anything that had happened before or focus on any of the pain that it brought. My stepsister, Autumn, had heard about the drama that had been going on with us. We talked a lot and she was always checking up on me to see how I was doing. I was her little butterfly.

She watched me grow from a little 12-year-old girl to a mother of three and a wife. She wasn't too happy about us getting married either, but she never judged me and stood by my side no matter what. Even though we weren't blood sisters, our bond says differently. She was definitely like the big sister I needed as a little girl growing up.

She had met Larry maybe once or twice. She thought he was okay but very funny because he loved to make people laugh. He also had a sweet side, my other siblings never really saw the bad side of him; they only heard about all of the stuff he had done to me.

Autumn called me up one night in the beginning of March, checking up on me and the kids. She also wanted to see how Larry and I were doing after the last big thing we had going on—him moving out for four months.

She told me that she felt that we needed to get away from Tallahassee for a while and come visit her. She had just moved to Atlanta, Georgia with her daughter Mia. Her sister Maya, my other stepsister, was already staying there with her husband and three children. I was more cool and close with Autumn than her. Now that she had moved closer was a blessing. Autumn moved from Fort Lauderdale, Florida. We haven't seen each other in a while, so Larry decided that Autumn was right.

"Let's take a trip to the A," he said!

I looked at him and said, "Yes, you're right."

It was a good idea because we needed a trip. Plus, it would be more like a family trip with the kids. We got up really early on that Friday and headed up to Atlanta. The ride was nice. We talked, laughed, and did our normal thing when we were on good terms. The kids slept most of the time. The ride wasn't long, about four-and-a-half hours. That was the kids and my first time going to Atlanta, so we were very excited.

We arrived at noon that Friday to Autumn's house. It was nothing but fun times when we linked up. We're 10 years different in age, but she was so down to earth. I loved her!

Anyway, we chilled, talked, laughed, drank, caught up on things and just enjoyed the moment. My other stepsister, her kids, and husband came over to chill with us too. Maya's husband and my husband clicked very well. My husband seemed to really like him and his vibes.

Throughout our stay, they took us around some of the city showing us a few things. My husband and I both liked the city on our first visit. It felt good to be around good people and a different environment then what we were used to. My brother-in-law told Larry that if he moved up to Atlanta, he could get him on at his job, and they were paying good. Larry had mentioned to him that Tallahassee doesn't pay well at those jobs.

Our weekend had come to an end so we had to head back to Florida. Before we left, Larry told them we might move up to Atlanta and my stepsister replied, "Come on."

On our way back to Tallahassee, Larry said he wanted to move to Atlanta. I looked at him and said, "Are you serious?"

He said "Yes, it's nothing in Tallahassee!"

I told him, "Let's do it."

By the end of May, we had found somewhere to stay and had moved all of our stuff into our new townhouse. It was said that some of our families on both sides were upset, sad, and some were happy. We had made the decision that moving to Atlanta would be a fresh start for our marriage and a great job opportunity for Larry.

We did what we thought was best for us. We officially moved to Atlanta June 3, 2011. Larry started work in July. My brother-in-law got him on with his job just like he had said. I decided not to work when we first moved to Atlanta. I needed a break, so I became a housewife. Larry was making great money, so we were fine.

I thought I'd let him cover all of the bills for a while and be the provider he's supposed to be. I needed a break. It felt good to just sit at home cook, clean, and get the boys to and from school. Everything seemed so perfect. It was a new city and state with no friends and barely any family. My household was finally in order and together. My daily routine was getting Larry to work and the boys to school.

My goal was to have the house clean by the time everybody got home. Larry wasn't going anywhere because he didn't know anybody, which was a good thing for us. There was no drama between us, we were just enjoying our new life. It all felt so different and much better than what we were use to back in Florida. All the drama we had in Tallahassee, you would've never known about it because it was like when we first met, spending time with each other and the kids. We even started going to church more.

I felt so blessed and happy that we made the move. We didn't let anyone stop us! After a year had passed, I decided to go back to work with the school board. Being at home became very boring. I don't see how real housewives do it. It didn't bother me to return back to work because I was used to it anyway. I'd never been the type to just sit home and do nothing. I had a job since I was 16 years old.

Things started getting a little hard because we only had one car. We needed another, and God blessed Larry to be able to get his first-time driver's license. So he bought his first car.

We were so excited! That was such a beautiful thing to see him be able to purchase his first car. I felt that God was really showing us so much favor. When he got his car, he was able to get home before me, so he would get the kids off the bus from school. They loved that.

A lot of people in my neighborhood acknowledged him always picking his kids up from the school bus. I was proud of him and I felt like we both were changing to make things work. My mother used to always call us and tell us how proud she was of us, his progress, and stepping up being the man of the household like he's supposed to be. She would make sure to let him know that God gave him that good job and financial blessing for a reason. She told him, "Don't mess up what God is doing in your life right now."

And he would tell her, "I know Ma, and I'm going to take care of my family."

It was a good feeling to hear him say that. After he got his car, he started hanging out with some coworkers. Which was cool because for a while when we first got to Atlanta, he was always in the house with the kids and I. But then it started getting to the point where he was staying out late.

I noticed him leaving every Friday after work. I started to worry because I felt that he was starting to find the same environment again. I brought it to his attention that he was starting to hang out a lot and coming in the house too late. He would always remind me that the first year we were in Atlanta he didn't go anywhere.

He started saying that a lot. To the point where I just felt like he was using it as an excuse. My attitude changed and he saw me acting the same way I used to in Tallahassee. I'd get mad and so upset about him hanging out all day and night. It's cool to hang out, but you don't have to be out all day and night when you have a family at home. In the blink of an eye, everything was back to how it was in Tallahassee.

The arguments were happening so frequently. He was gone all day, staying out late all night and wouldn't call. Things got so unstable in our house, and it was very noticeable when we went out around other people. I was finding myself being mad, angry, and so frustrated. I tried to put my focus on my children or something else, but that seemed to be my only focus. Then I was wondering what he was out doing and who he was doing it with.

I used to call his phone, and sometimes I would try to be nice so he would come home. That's all I ever wanted; just my family and him of course. It never worked, so I would start going off on him and texting his phone and sending all kinds of pissed off text messages. I would tell him that I'm his wife and these are his kids and he shouldn't be gone all day and night. He would tell me, "Don't tell me what to do. I'm grown."

I used to explain to him, "It doesn't matter if you're grown or not. You are married. Things change when you get married, and not just for you but for me as well. You cannot continue to do all of the stuff you used to do when you're married." He wasn't listening to anything I was saying, and he didn't care. It went in one ear and out of the other one. One day we would be okay, and the next one it would be a big argument between us. We weren't seeing eye-to-eye at all. He wasn't spending any time with me or the kids anymore. It's sad how things could change so fast from good to bad.

My moods changed and he didn't care. It got to the point that by the time I got home from work, he was already dressed and gone. I wouldn't see him all day or night. I would sit up and wait for him all night to come home. There were lots of sleepless nights from me staying up waiting for him to get there. Five and six o'clock in the morning would come, and I would still be waiting... but nothing.

I used to call his phone and text him but I'd get no answer or reply. I would call back to back to see if he would answer or hopefully know where he was at. He would get so pissed at me for doing that and tell me how childish I was, but it didn't matter to me. I just wanted him to come home and not be out cheating on me.

I started doing whatever I could so he wouldn't cheat because I knew that's what he was out doing. He would get phone calls, and when he answered, he would yell in the phone, "HELLO? HELLO?", then hang it up. Next, call one of his homeboys right after to make it seem like it was them. But my instinct was always right.

I used to see his call log and some text messages from chicks all of the time. Even naked pictures from people I knew and some were family members. It would upset me but I would just go out and buy him something, make us dinner and put on some sexy lingerie.

I was thinking that maybe what I was doing wasn't enough and I needed to do more. I changed the way I dressed and hairstyles frequently for him. I noticed the girls he was always messing with and how they dressed, so I figured maybe I needed to dress like that. I even got lashes put on, but when I would do those things, he never liked it on me at all. No one knew how insecure I was about everything.

My self-esteem was so low that you wouldn't imagine. There were times that I didn't say anything at all. I would just let him hang out all night, even if it killed me, just so he could see that I'm cool and okay with it. On top of being his wife, I was trying to be his friend too. I was only hurting myself, but I just wanted him to be happy, love me and want to be with me. I didn't really have to tell my friends how I felt or what was going on in my household, but they could tell.

They didn't like the way he treated me from the beginning, and they felt moving to Atlanta with him was a big mistake. I lost and gained so many friendships through out my entire relationship with Larry!!

One night he left the house and didn't come back home. I called his phone all night and morning. At noon, he answered the phone and said he was up at the barbershop. I asked him why he didn't come home last night. He said he fell asleep at his coworkers house. He didn't call or anything when he woke up, and I knew he had seen my calls. This started happening a lot—from staying out late to not coming home, and not answering my calls or text messages.

He would say that he didn't have service but I would see him on social media all night. I really started fussing all of the time, nagging because I was getting tired of him doing the things he was doing. I would tell him, "If you did what you were supposed to do and be the man of the house and husband like your supposed to, there wouldn't be anything to fuss about."

He was living a single life while we were married. The kids weren't included in any of his activities or daily routines either.

The kids were always with me; everywhere they went or anything they did was with me. He would just leave us in the house. He would tell me I needed to start hanging out too so I wouldn't bother him or fuss so much. But we didn't move to Atlanta for that. We got into a big argument in the car one day and he mushed-my head into the window in front of the kids.

I jumped out of the car and started walking. I don't know what was going on with our marriage, but it was a mess, and I was putting up with so much. His temper was awful, and so was his drinking. He became a very selfish person to me. His friends and family members couldn't see it; everyone thought it was me. But he treated everybody differently than he treated me. Whenever I was alone I would sit in the closet or shower and just cry.

I cried so much it was ridiculous. I had lost so much weight; my weight was always up and down. It was very noticeable. But, like always, I would apologize to him for everything, even if it wasn't my fault. I always tried to make things right. I even saw in his Facebook account how he was inboxing people he used to mess with and they were entertaining him, knowing he was married.

But hey, it didn't matter to them because they weren't married to me. One of my little cousins was in his inbox as well. He was asking her for pictures of her private parts. I even found out that every time we went to Florida to visit, he was sleeping with females during our visits. Of course I got upset and locked him out of his account because I wanted him to know I saw everything.

Later on that night, we got into a huge fight when he was about to leave to go hang out or whatever he was doing. I asked him about the Facebook account and text messages. He told me not to question him. That he was grown and he could do whatever he wanted. It never failed with me bringing up the fact that we were married. Either he really didn't understand that or he just didn't care.

Things got out of hand with our tones while yelling at each other. The kids were downstairs and we were upstairs. My sister Lisa, was there that night because she had come to stay with me for a while. She heard us upstairs but she didn't say anything. He tried to get all of his clothes out of the house so he could go stay at his coworker's house. He was always telling me I got on his nerves when I asked questions or tried to talk to him about our problems.

I stood in front of him and told him he wasn't leaving out the room until we finished talking. That surely touched a nerve because he ran in the closet and grabbed his gun. He put it in my face and told me if I didn't move he was going to shoot me and didn't care about the kids being downstairs. I told him I was tired of him pulling the gun on me and that I was about to call the police.

He took my phone and broke it. I opened my room door and yelled downstairs and told my sister to call the police. She did, and before the police could get there, I took his phone and wouldn't give it back. Things escalated and the police arrived. I didn't tell them about the gun. I just told them we got into a bad argument. They made him leave for the night. But once again, I would reach out to him the next day because he would never call or text me.

I would go out and buy him something, get lingerie, cook dinner, get him some liquor and even Google different sex positions. I was trying to do whatever I could to make him happy and make everything go away. I took care of the kids and everything that had to do with them, just so he wouldn't be bothered with anything. That didn't stop him from doing the things he was doing. It didn't matter if I fussed or was quiet. He had really gotten out of hand with doing whatever he wanted to do. Every weekend he would be gone Friday, Saturday, and Sunday.

Like always, he was at a "coworker's" house and his phone didn't have service. Even when we would get into an argument he would grab some clothes and go stay the night with this coworker. And I let him. Whenever he came back home, I would have sex with him to take his mind off things but one week I thought we were having a good week, no arguments or anything.

I was like a mouse around the house because I didn't want to piss him off or make him want to leave. He never did anything to make me happy, even during my silence. But just when I thought things were good because of my silence around the house, I got a text one day while we were both at work. From him saying he was moving out that Friday and he thought it was best.

I went mental and was begging him not to leave, to please stay. I told him I would change whatever it is he want me to change and I would do better, when in reality I was just trying to be the best wife I could be for him. I tried to keep our family together, but he moved out anyway. We had only been in Atlanta for two years and our marriage was a disaster. I was so hurt that he was moving out. It was killing me that he just up and moved out on me. He claimed he was moving in with a coworker, and later I found out that this coworker he was always hollering about was a woman. I should've known better!

There was no way he was always out chilling with some homeboys, and I knew he wasn't always staying over some guys' house. By the time I found out the coworker was another woman, mostly everybody in Florida already knew. This was one of the most frustrating things ever in my life. It was hard for me to deal with that, especially because we were married.

I couldn't trust the marriage situation enough and I was tired of saying it myself. I called and texted his phone because I knew the sudden move he did was already planned. How do you just up and leave your wife and kids in a whole new state and city. Not only did he suddenly move out; he stopped giving me money and helping out with anything. When I called him for money, he would tell me he's not giving me anything. To me, he was still responsible for helping pay bills and taking care of the kids no matter where he moved to.

But he was trying to be spiteful towards me. I couldn't get any help or money from him at all. He just didn't caring about us at the moment. I went to the courthouse to figure out what to do, but they claimed they couldn't give out that kind of advice in Gwinnett County. I was aggravated!

When I was leaving the courthouse, an officer was driving around in the parking lot and stopped and asked me was I okay. I told him, "No."

Then he asked, "What were you trying to get help with?"

I told him the situation and he said, "Hold on, my friend is a judge."

He called his friend while I was standing there and told him everything I told him. When he got off the phone he wrote down a number I needed to call. He told me I needed to file for abandonment because we were still married and he just moved out and hadn't given me any money for the kids. I didn't want to do that, but I had no other choice but to go file for abandonment .

I filed for the abandonment and we went to court. The judge ordered him to pay a certain amount of money until we got our divorce and child support going. Larry was mad. All my stressing and depression had come back stronger than ever.

I was basically taking care of three kids on my own. He had stopped getting our son from the bus stop and all. I tried to use the kids to get him to talk to me, come over to the house, or to give me money, but none of that worked with him. That woman had him locked and in loved with her. I was torn into pieces with him moving in with another woman. I felt my life was over and I didn't have enough strength to go forward every day. It had me so sick to my stomach.

I knew I had to focus and still take care of my kids, and I did, but that had a big part of me down every day and night. We went without talking for weeks and months. Finally, he started coming back over and around. Here goes me sending out a text to him saying, "Good Morning, baby," "I miss you," and "Please come back."

I would even text him and tell him the kids missed him. I sent nude pictures and videos trying to get him to come back home. On our anniversary, March 19, 2014, I sent him a card in the mail to her house and put "To My Husband" on the card. I didn't care at all and I wanted to piss her off. He never acknowledged the card, but I'm sure they got it. When him and her would get into it, I would let him move back in. I knew they still worked together and were going to still communicate.

I just wanted him there and was accepting of any and everything he was doing. I was trying to keep it all together because I was extremely hurt on the inside. Once him and her made up, he would move back out again with her and ignore me. One Saturday, the kids and I went out to eat on Valentine's Day at Bahama Breeze restaurant. While we were eating, my son Romelo said, "Isn't that Larry?"

We all turned and looked out the window, and it was him and her coming into the same restaurant. He had just sent me a text five minutes before telling me, "Happy Valentines Day." He said he loved and missed the kids and I. My heart was beating so fast when I saw them together. On the way out of the restaurant, I made sure he saw his kids and I. He was nothing but a manipulator, not only to me but to her as well. Hard as it was, I didn't want the kids to be a part of the confusion we had going on, so I would allow them to go over and stay there with him on weekends.

A lot of people thought that was crazy of me, but I didn't want them to be put in the middle. It was up to him to explain to them what was going on. He got pulled over by the police one night after he left my house telling me how I better not have another man around his kids. All while he was staying with another woman. He threatened me with his gun and told me to try him and see what happened.

My homegirl Tisha was there, and she told him he can't run my house while he was doing his own thing. He looked at me, then he got in his car and left. He had been drinking, and I know how he can be when he's drinking. I went to sleep and I woke up the next day to find out that he had gone to jail that night. He got pulled over for a DUI. They took his car and gun. I was relieved to find out they took the gun and that he wasn't getting that back. I told him I was going to file for a divorce. We both agreed to it.

I told everyone I was done and I'm going to file. I didn't have the money for a lawyer and I reached out to legal aid, but it took forever for them to help. I had never filed before and didn't have any assistance. My stepsister, Autumn, told me I could do it myself, just Google the paperwork for divorce in my county. That's what I did and then filed for the divorce.

Right after I did that, him and the girl got into it. He moved back in with me and I did a dismissal for the divorce. We were okay, but I guess it was hard for him to not mess with the woman since they worked together. I don't know. I was trying to figure things out because they got back together and then he was upset that I had dismissed the divorce. He was back and forth from us both, and we both allowed this foolishness to go on. He was my husband, so what else was I supposed to do. My mother was bothered by this whole situation. Nobody could understand why either one of us kept going back to each other.

At times, I thought I was ready, then at times I wasn't. All of this had my body aching everywhere and me constantly going to the doctor. He moved out again and I started having problems with my stomach. The doctor told me I had a hernia in my stomach. Every time I strained, the hernia would push through a hole that was a weakened part of my muscle in my stomach. I had to have surgery on my stomach, a hernia repair to get the hole covered up. Soon as I found out, I called to let him know about everything. He told me to keep him posted like he was concern, but I could hear her in the background. That hernia was giving me so many problems. Since we were still married I was under his health insurance. I called him to inform him about my surgery and asked him if he could watch the kids. He told me no and that he was going to Florida for his sister's graduation. Which, of course, started an argument. He hung up the phone on me too. I felt it was mostly because of her but his attitude toward me was horrendous. I was so upset and didn't care about anything he was saying because we had previously talked about this already.

When I got to the hospital to have my surgery, they told me I didn't have health insurance. I looked at the lady and said, "Yes I do. I'm covered under my husband's health insurance. I just went to my doctor's appointment to schedule the surgery a couple days ago."

They kept trying to check me in and run my insurance but it kept showing that I didn't have any. I didn't know what was going on. I was already nervous about having the surgery and my nerves were extremely bad. I had to get out of line and call the insurance company to find out that I was removed by Larry off of the health insurance the day before. I couldn't do anything but damn near pull my hair out from being annoyed and angry. Luckily, they told me to not worry about it.

They were still going to do my surgery, but just bill me directly instead. I couldn't believe someone would do that to their wife and kids' mother. Months after my surgery, I went and filed for another divorce, just to turn around and have that one dismissed as well! Everything was repeated with us. Nothing changed and nothing was new! I was kind of numb to all of that. I was like the walking dead. That's how I truly felt every day.

Larry and the other woman got into an argument and he ended up going to jail again. That time he had the kids over there with them. That was one of the worst nights of my kids' lives and mine. They were so terrified, and so was I when I got the call from the police. Of course, I had to go get him out of jail, but his sister paid for it. I was overly stressed, and with all of this, my hair started falling out, my face and arms were breaking out so badly, and I had lost so much weight.

I went to the doctor about my skin and they told me I was breaking out from emotional stress. He prescribed me different kinds of creams and antibiotics. I asked him how much was that going to cost because I didn't have any health insurance. I told him my situation with my husband taking me off of his insurance without telling me. The dermatologist ended up not charging me for the visit. He saw how disturbed I was. He gave me free medication and didn't charge me for the visit. One of my homegirl's was hurting from the things I was going through and how I was looking at work.

She introduced me to one of her guy friends to help me focus on someone else and try to get my mind off things. But that didn't last or work for me because I didn't want to be doing the same thing he was doing. I didn't want to commit adultery too.

The back and forth was still going on. He went to jail for the third time because they were fighting again. I had to go get him out once more.
That was so embarrassing, going to see my husband and picking him up from jail. Also because of the fact that he's in

there for fighting with his girlfriend. When I arrived to the jail house, I had to show my I.D. because the officer asked who I was. I explained that I was his wife. She replied, "And he is here for fighting his girlfriend?!"

I looked at her like she was crazy and I couldn't believe she had said that to me, but, she was right and she was looking at me like I was crazy. My life and household were messed up. My oldest son got to the point where he would stay in his room all day and only come down to eat. When he got in from football practice after school, he would eat and go straight to his room, close the door and wouldn't come back out.

He wasn't saying anything to Larry anymore unless Larry said something to him. I started to see hurt in my son eyes. One day, I called him into my room and sat him down. He told me that he didn't like Larry, he didn't want him there, Larry didn't do anything for them, that I did everything and I kept letting him back in the house. My son was only 15 years old telling me this. I felt horrible because I was hurting not only myself, but my kids too.

To hear my son say that was enough for me. No one could understand why I was putting myself through all of that. I didn't really know the answers anymore. God was allowing him to hurt me over and over again until I woke up. Everything that was happening to him was karma. He lost a good-paying job and two cars.

I couldn't take it anymore. I had to give it up. I went and filed a third time for a divorce. This time I went through with it. He had no idea because I didn't even let him know.

CHAPTER 10
LESSONS & BLESSINGS

Things were a mess in my life. I went and filed for a divorce. I was at my breaking point. So many things had happened, and I couldn't take it anymore. Divorce is something no one would want to experience. When you get married, you don't think about ever getting divorced. Larry and I weren't fully prepared or mature enough for marriage, but I didn't think we would ever divorce.

With all the trouble he was getting in with the law, and us going back and forth, I finally left him alone. During the process of it all, I decided to go back to school and get my high school diploma on September 24, 2014. I wanted to do something to make me feel good about myself and to achieve my goals. Our divorce was finalized on December 10, 2014, and I was given full custody of our boys.

He disagreed with joint custody because he claimed he couldn't have the kids that much, so the judge ordered him to get the kids every other weekend and visitation on holidays between 2-8 p.m., if I wanted to. I was hoping for joint custody because I thought it was only right that he spent as much time with the kids as I did.

He was also ordered to pay monthly child support. We went our separate ways after that. He wasn't happy at all about the child support amount, so he didn't give the kids anything for Christmas. Of course, he blames everything on me, per usual. A couple of months after the divorce, we started back messing around. The female he was messing with had put him out or he moved out, whichever one.

I even let him move back in because he didn't have any place to go. He had to do a couple of months in jail for the mess he had created during his adultering. He wrote me letters telling me how much he was sorry for everything he had done to me: pulling the gun on me, all the cheating, and disrespect. He said that I was a beautiful angel from God sent to him. It seemed like jail talk, but I believed that he was really sorry because he had never told me he was sorry for anything he's ever done to me. We even talked about getting remarried when he got out. He said that the drinking had him acting like that and doing the things he was doing.

I thought that could be true. After his couple of months was up in jail, he came back and stayed with us. I wasn't sure if I really wanted to do that, but I still loved him, and he was my kids' dad. He had to find a temp job because his other job wouldn't hire him back with his charges and because the previous girlfriend still worked there. Things were very awkward between us like we were trying to force something. All of the things that he'd done to me would constantly play in my mind.

I used to question myself all of the time, like why would I even still communicate with this man. After everything that he'd done to me and all the humiliation he put me through, why was I letting him stay in my house? Even all the humiliation I put myself through as well. Other guys would say, "You're a good person because a lot of women wouldn't do the stuff you do after all he's done to you."

Those things played in my head so much. The sex wasn't the same and it's like I didn't want to be around him anymore. The judge ordered him to do anger management classes, and I didn't want to give him a ride to that. It's like everything was hitting me. He'd lost everything over this other woman and got all those charges but wanted me to help him. God was seriously punishing him for all the adultery/infidelity that he'd done.

He betrayed our marriage and partnership. I was in a place where I agreed with God and I wanted him to feel all the pain I felt. I wanted him to hurt the way I was hurting. I was always there for him no matter what happened, what he did or who he did it with. It wasn't my job to get him to and from work or to anger management and back. If he hadn't betrayed our marriage, he would still have everything.

He still was doing disrespectful stuff in my house after he got out of jail—talking with and texting girls. It was just too toxic for the both of us. I told him that I was moving out my townhouse and he couldn't move with me, so he moved back to Florida. Everything about us was damaged, and there was no fixing anything.

When he left it was supposed to have been a happy moment, but it wasn't. I was even more sad and depressed than before. I was missing him and was having moments asking myself if I really wanted for him to leave the state. I knew everything involving the kids was going to be on me, which the majority of the time it was anyway.

When he moved, I felt endless pain that just wouldn't go away. My emotions were all over the place. When I found out he was messing with people in Florida, I let that get to me. I still would sit up crying, not being able to eat, over-thinking everything. He was always nonchalant about everything and I was extra. My feelings always got the best of me when it came down to Larry. I would worry who he was with and what he was doing. He came to visit one Thanksgiving, and we messed around. Also, I went to Florida one weekend for Christmas, and we messed around. He had gotten into a whole new relationship and it was all over the internet.

I would still send nude pictures, call, and text, trying to get his attention because I didn't fully want to let go like I thought I would've. Even though we were divorced. Sometimes he would ignore me, and sometimes he wouldn't. I even thought about moving back to Florida to be with my family. I was having major withdrawals.

My cousin kayliah, would tell me that I needed to just let him go and move forward with my life. Don't move back to Florida, stay in Georgia. He's moved on with his life, you need to do the same. It's going to hurt because y'all have history, but it's time for you to move on. It's going to take time, but God is going to heal you. She told me it may seem like you're not ever going to get over the pain or him, but you will. My homegirl used to tell me the same thing and even told me to get me a guy friend again to help take my mind off him and to help me heal.

One day, I just cried and prayed out to God. I told him I was tired, overwhelmed, emotionally drained, and wanted to be free. I cried and asked God to break this chain between Larry and I. I repeated this prayer every day, every second, minute and hour. I found myself and Romelo, a psychologist to go see for a couple of months just to make sure we were both okay. I didn't want Larry Jr. and Ross to go because I felt they were too young. Talking with them about some things was enough for them.

This was a great idea because I saw a change in Romelo. He opened up so much to the psychologist. I didn't put it out to the world that we were going, but my mother knew. This helped so much, and I recommend this for anyone who needs it. It's always good to talk to someone who knows nothing about you or your situation and they just listen to you. I'm not ashamed of going, and I'm glad I made that step. I wanted and needed all of the help I could get because I was serious about my healing and letting go of the past.

Also, I started talking to this guy to try to also help take the thoughts and pain away, which was my homegirl Natalie's advice! That didn't work because when I talked to him it seemed fake. I wasn't into it at all. We even went to dinner and I was ready to go home immediately. I prayed out to God again and told him, "Lord, only you can help me, nobody else can. I don't want to use anyone to help me through this pain but you."

I stopped answering my phone for the dude and cut him off completely. I stopped texting and calling Larry, and I wasn't sending any more pictures.

I downloaded daily devotional and inspirational apps to my phone. I would read them every day, all day, and listen to either Gospel or chill instrumental music. I stopped talking about Larry completely. I even got off social media. It was so hard, but I prayed every day and was taking it one day at a time. Some days were good, and some were bad. I knew I had to keep moving forward and couldn't go backward.

I barely talked to him about the kids because I knew I was still emotional, plus very vulnerable. I did as little communicating with him as possible. Slowly but surely I was finding my way.

Throughout my healing process someone we both knew passed away. I went to the funeral and prepared myself to face him. I actually did better then what I thought. I spoke to him, and that's about it, nothing else. When I left the funeral, I didn't even have the hunger to text him or call him the whole time I was in town. I knew then that my prayers were working. I felt so good about myself. Nobody would ever understand that feeling. From that day forward, I knew I was okay. Every day got better and better. I still had some weak days and moments but I kept pushing myself forward. I disconnected from his family and they did the same. My prayers were working; God heard my cry. Although my weight was still up and down.

My kids were seeing a better side of me. Larry had been in Florida for one year at that point. I started making changes within myself for myself, focusing more on myself and my kids and not worrying about my past and things that had happened. I was trying to find solutions to fix things that the devil tried to destroy. I eventually stopped going to see the psychologist. Our kids were doing well. My baby boy still had his moments about his daddy not being in the house. He kept asking, "Is daddy coming back and when?"

Him and I were riding in the car when he asked, "Mommy, can you please let daddy come back?"

I was caught by surprise with that one. I knew how he felt about his dad, but I never thought he would say that. It made me feel sad and bad because he said it as if Mommy was the reason daddy wasn't there. Obviously, that wasn't the case at all. It really touched me, but I told him, "Your dad is not coming back to stay, but he will come to visit. You can call him anytime if you want to."

I knew he didn't quite understand, but it was on my mind for the rest of the night. You never want them to have to choose, pick sides, or even put them in the middle. I had to grow and mature on that note. In all reality, my kids were damaged too by all of this. I prayed for our communication and co-parenting. The good thing about God he knows our struggle and he knows what needs to be done.

I knew I needed more income for the boys and I. Going back to school to get a degree had never been an option for me. At times, I wanted to leave the school board and sometimes I didn't. I was still a bus monitor and that wasn't enough pay for me. I prayed to God to lead me in the right direction for a new job or new position.

God laid it on my heart to go get my CDL license and become a bus driver. I thought, *A bus driver? I'm scared to drive my car on 85, let alone a bus.*

Well, I did exactly what God told me to do even though I really didn't want to. I studied for my CDLs and passed the test. Then I became a bus driver and have been driving for nearly three years. All I ever think about is my kids. Everything I do is for them. Starting to love myself more and knowing my worth was well overdue. I cut one of our close friends, Levi, off because I didn't want to associate with anyone that was close to him.

During my healing process, I wanted to be clear from anything that involved him, besides our kids. It was just something I felt I had to do for me. Things were really looking better for me. I was smiling and laughing more, enjoying waking up every morning and going to church every Sunday. I spent all of my time with the kids and doing different things. It was all about us now, and my oldest son couldn't be happier.

I was writing in my book more and more and reading my word nonstop! I was enjoying my job as a bus driver too. I socialized more in my neighborhood, job, and children's football teams and connected with some beautiful families who cherish my boys and I. My attitude has definitely changed and I was ignoring a lot of things. I never thought I would see the day that I left Larry alone or we left each other alone.

I just knew that's how my life was going to be forever. But God saw differently and was just waiting on me to mean what I say and to really want what I'm asking for.

My weight had gone back up and my skin cleared up into a beautiful glow. I prayed for women and girls all over the world that they never have to go through what I went through.

If you're in a relationship or marriage and it's toxic, please get out of it. Don't stay and don't accept anything if it's not real love. God doesn't want you to be with someone or married to anyone if you're not happy and being abused. Make sure you understand what *till death do us apart* and *for better or for worse* means. God doesn't want you to be anywhere where you're not happy.

If you're married, never take advice from someone who isn't married or has never been married. Instead, listen to God!! He will hear your cry and prayers. There are some people that say I wasn't a good wife but that doesn't matter to me.

Don't ever get so caught up in a relationship or marriage that you lose yourself. I was like a dead man walking for so long, and now that I'm on the other side, I know what I deserve. Love yourself first, and it doesn't matter if it's your kids' dad. I allowed myself to be pulled into places and situations I never should've been in.

I loved a man more than I loved myself. Your husband comes before your children in a marriage, but I went about it the wrong way. I regret that my kids were a part of and had to go through that as well. I learned so much from my past relationship. No man should ever mentally or physically abuse you and vice versa! Never give a man power over you to treat you however he wants to. Believe in yourself and don't be afraid to walk away.

Tenica Cofield

Always continue to have self-respect. So many times I go to the park and lift my arms up like a bird, close my eyes and pretend I'm flying when the wind blows. I say, "Thank God I am Free."

God has someone out there just for you who is going to treat you like the queen you are. When he made one man, he made another. A lot of people doubt me and my situation because they loved him so much, but you should never look past the truth just because of how much you love someone. At times, I wonder if all of this happened to me because of how I did my friend, Chloe, and my cousin, Nicole.

I honestly use to think God was punishing me, but it was nothing but a lesson. God was trying to tell me I needed to repent and do things differently. I didn't listen then, but I'm all ears now, and it's never too late. My marriage had broken me. Then, BOOM, God healed me!

LIVING FREE

I've come a long way. I'm nowhere near the person I used to be, and I'm glad. A change is huge and hard to do. We often get so comfortable with who we are or what we're used too. Sometimes we want to change but don't know how to or worry if others are going to accept our change. But we must change for God and ourselves, not others. I spent so much time trying to figure out things that were out of my control and trying to explain things that didn't need an explanation. "Let God do the talking," is what I tell myself now.

I used to go back and forth with people. I was always in defensive mode. I've talked about people and people talked about me. Lots of friendships have come and gone, also a relationship and marriage! Nothing lasts when God says it's over. I didn't lose anything or anyone. God removed it all for me. There is nothing God removed that I want back because I know he's replacing everything and everyone with something greater. Certain things and people are seasonal.

Some things last forever and some don't, and we must know that it's a part of life. I've learned that everyone can't go with you where God is taking you. I love everyone dearly, and I pray for everyone that has crossed my path and played major roles in my life. Some may see my growth and some may not, but God does. We all outgrow a lot of things like our ways, friendships, relationships, and jobs. We can't sit around dwelling on it or the past. We must move on and let go. I love my growth, maturity, and strength. It took me a long time to get here but I'm here to stay. It took me more than five years to write this book. I started, then I'd stop, and started it again, then I stopped because I was so scared, ashamed, very much embarrassed by the things that happened to me, and frightened about what others would think.

People are always saying, "Oh she's playing victim," or this and that.

I'm not a victim. I'm a SURVIVOR! The purpose of me writing this book is to help others, encourage women/girls, and let them know they're not alone. I know how it feels to feel alone and hold everything inside. I want girls and women all across the world to tell their story. Your story matters, and it's important. People need to hear how God brought you through every obstacle in life.

Don't be afraid to share, and don't let naysayers discourage you from doing what you want. I didn't write this book to put others down or to make anyone look bad, not even myself. This was a healing process and encouragement for me. My book is to let my readers know that I am human, I made mistakes, and lived through lots of bad decisions. I go through stuff and hurt just like them. I've been broke, stressed, depressed, lonely, and miserable. I'm not perfect and my life isn't, nor has it ever been peaches and cream. No one can tell my STORY, but me. That's why we should never judge a book by its cover.

I was taught that no matter what you go through in life when you step out that door, hold your head high, dress well, smile and don't ever look like what you're going through. I will always carry that with me, and I will teach my three boys the same. Some family members and outsiders judge me so much based off of what they thought they knew. I heard so many times, "She thinks she's all of that," "She thinks she's perfect," "She acts like she just has it all together," and "She's trying to live beyond her means." Along with, "That's what she gets."

All I'm trying to do is live my best life like everyone else does. It doesn't matter where I come from. That doesn't define who I am. My past will never ever define my future. My strength offends people, but they don't know that I've had plenty of weak moments.

I wrote this book to give you the real me and my real life. People think they know me, but they have no idea, well until after reading this book. If you've known me all of my life, you still don't know me because I grow and change daily. I use to regret things. Now I don't. Everything is a lesson and a blessing. Holding dead weight, grudges, pain, and guilt only hinder you from blessings, peace, and living life.

I forgive every one that hurt me. I prayed and asked God to forgive me for those I hurt, even my children. Most of the things I did was out of character or because I was hurting. I'm seeing days, places, people, and things I thought I would never see. I am a 37 -year-old mother raising three handsome boys and teaching them how to be men of God, kings, leaders, providers and wonderful husbands.

My first son recently graduated from high school in 2018, and now he's doing his Sophomore year of college at Middle

Tenica Cofield

Georgia State University. I'm a great mother, and my heart beats for myself and my children.

I couldn't be more proud of the person I am today. It's all through the grace of God, my children, and my mother. My mother has played a major role in my life. I don't know where I would be without her by my side ever since I entered this world. She is an amazing woman of God, mother, and grandmother. I admire her strength, and I'm blessed beyond measure to say I get it from her. She taught me how to do the most important thing in life, and that's pray.

The best thing any parent can teach their children is how to pray. There's nothing like a praying mother and woman. I took left turns but prayer took me back to the right. As you have read, so many things have happened in my life. Some can relate and some cannot. We all go through different things and it affects us all differently.

Throughout my life, I went through so many trials and tribulations. From birth, I thought that I would never be the same as everyone else or fit in. I lived behind the unknown for many years. I used that as an excuse to stay stuck somewhere I didn't want to be. Living behind fear is so dangerous, and it only damages you mentally.

I was tired and I knew it was time for me to become something else. My stepsister, Autumn, started calling me "Butterfly" years ago and I didn't understand why. Now, I know exactly why, and I appreciate her for letting me know WHO I WAS. She saw the transformation in me long before I did. I was that caterpillar who was afraid to transform into something more

156

beautiful. I am free, stronger, wiser, happier, and peaceful!

This is a lovely place to be in, and I owe it all to God, my support team and my prayer warriors. I'm not fully committed to God as I should be, but I'm on my way. I pray more daily, write more daily, and read my bible more daily. That's the beauty of my life now.

"LORD, I THANK YOU."

When I finally took that step, my life changed and I blossomed into this GORGEOUS BUTTERFLY!!!

Bitter to better! Fearful to fearless! Ugly to pretty! Sad to happy! Weak to strong! Bothered to unbothered! Dead to alive! Wise to wiser! Stressed to blessed! Drained to regained! Dead to living free!

"She is clothed with strength and dignity and she laughs without fear of the future."

Proverbs 31:25(NLT)

Tenica Cofield

CPSIA information can be obtained
at www.ICGtesting.com
Printed in the USA
BVHW050144250720
584505BV00005B/29